Exercises for
Understanding
English Grammar

Exercises for
Understanding
English Grammar

FOURTH EDITION

Martha Kolln

The Pennsylvania State University

Robert Funk

Eastern Illinois University

New York San Francisco Boston
London Toronto Sydney Tokyo Singapore Madrid
Mexico City Munich Paris Cape Town Hong Kong Montreal

ISBN 0-321-31682-7

6 7 8 9 10—ML—08

Contents

Chapter 6
Modifiers of the Noun: Adjectivals 81

Preface

The fourth edition of *Exercises for Understanding English Grammar* follows the goals and design of the previous editions: to provide additional practice and supplemental instruction for users of *Understanding English Grammar*. The exercises in this book will enable students to reinforce their grasp of basic concepts, to extend and explore their understanding, and to apply their knowledge to their writing.

This edition of *Exercises* is designed to accompany *Understanding English Grammar*, 7th Edition; it follows the organization of that text. Some of the exercises replicate the format of those in the main text, but many take a different approach, challenging students to demonstrate their grammatical competence by combining, composing, and revising sentences. Although most of the chapters review key points and provide additional examples, students are expected to learn grammatical principles by studying the parent text itself. References to the sentence patterns and sentence slots, for example, depend upon the information in Chapter 2 of *Understanding English Grammar*.

New to this fourth edition is Chapter 11 on Purposeful Punctuation, which supplements the material in the new Chapter 15 of the main text. In addition there are new exercises on linking verbs (Chapter 2), on dangling and misplaced modifiers (Chapter 6), and on heteronyms (Chapter 10). A number of other exercises have been revised and updated.

We have retained the self-instructional feature of *Exercises for Understanding English Grammar* by including the answers to all the items in Chapter 1 and to the odd-numbered items for most of the other exercises. We do not supply answers for the composing and sentence-combining exercises, but we do offer suggested responses for exercises that involve revising faulty sentences. Chapters 2 through 10 also have summary "test" exercises at the end, for which no answers are included. Answers that are not given here can be found in the accompanying Answer Key.

We think that *Exercises for Understanding English Grammar* will provide valuable support for you and your students. We are grateful for the helpful comments of Rebecca Argall, University of Memphis; Rosemary Buck, Eastern Illinois University; Dennis Burges, Longwood University; John Hagge, Iowa State University; Leon Heaton, University of Memphis; Duangrudi Suksang, Eastern Illinois University; and Beth Rapp Young, University of Central Florida at Orlando. We welcome further criticisms and suggestions for making this book even more useful to you.

Martha Kolln

Robert Funk

Chapter 1

Grammar, Usage, and Language Change

As the Introduction to Part I of *Understanding English Grammar* points out, you are already an expert in using your native language. You have the competence both to create and to understand sentences that you have never heard or read. If you have reached this point on the page and understood what you have read, you "know" English grammar.

The five exercises in this first chapter are designed to help you explore your innate understanding of grammar: to recognize some basic principles of sentence structure, to understand the difference between *describing* language and *prescribing* its usage, and to look at the way that the language changes.

GRAMMATICALITY

Your knowledge of grammar is something you developed with little conscious effort as a child. You learned how to put words together in the right order, and you acquired the ability to recognize when a string of words is not grammatical. For example, read the following sentences and rate them according to their acceptability:

1. Old this wooden shack is over falling almost.

2. This wooden old shack is falling almost over.

3. This old wooden shack is almost falling over.

Chances are you have rated them, in order of acceptability, 3, 2, and 1. If you examine why you accepted the third and rejected the first, you will discover some rules that are part of your language competence—rules about word order and movability.

Exercise 1.1
Determining Grammatical Structure

Directions: Rearrange the following words to form grammatical sentences (use only the words given). It might be possible to make more than one grammatical arrangement.

1. Ring bells loudly the.

   _____

2. I gave a book my sister.

   _____

3. Mary should stop smoking is clear that.

   _____

4. Tigers six of the jungle ran out.

   _____

5. Ship sails the today.

   _____

6. For green its age my well car runs old.

   _____

7. She owns many birdcages antique beautiful.

   _____

DESCRIPTIVE AND PRESCRIPTIVE RULES

The previous exercise showed that you know which combinations of words are grammatical in English and which are not. The rule, or principle, that says whether a sentence is grammatical or not is a **descriptive** rule: It describes the way native speakers structure their language. The validity of a descriptive rule depends on whether the combination of words is possible in English, and the evidence to support the rule comes from the knowledge that native speakers of English have (even if that knowledge is largely unconscious) and from samples of their actual use of the language.

People speaking the same language sometimes disagree in their evaluation of particular sentences. For example, some speakers of English would find "The baby needs changed" acceptable, while others might think it odd and would say instead "The baby needs changing" or "The baby needs to be changed." A number of differences in the use of English have acquired social importance, and some people think that certain uses are "ungrammatical" and mark their users as uneducated. Rules that tell people which usages to adopt or avoid are called **prescriptive** rules. Most of us tend to pay greater attention to prescriptive rules when we are on our best linguistic behavior, especially when we are writing in a formal style.

Exercise 1.2

Identifying Rules

Directions: Briefly explain whether the following rules are descriptive or prescriptive.

1. Articles (*a, an,* and *the*) precede nouns.

2. Do not use unnecessary words.

3. In questions, the verb usually begins the sentence.

4. Avoid frequent use of *be* as a main verb.

5. You may use "It's me" in speech.

6. Imperative sentences (e.g., "Leave at once") usually lack a subject.

7. Adverbs such as *however* can be moved around in sentences.

8. Do not use the passive voice without a good reason.

9. Most verbs form the past tense by adding *-d* or *-ed* to the base form.

10. Use precise adjectives and concrete nouns.

STANDARD AND NONSTANDARD ENGLISH

When we speak of "good grammar" or "proper usage," we are talking about the **standard** variety, or dialect, of a language. Standard English is the variety that carries the most prestige, mainly because it is associated with education and professional success. It is also the version that normally appears in print. In fact, standard American English is often called "edited American English," because the final or "edited" draft of a written work is expected to conform to this version. People are also expected to use standard English in college coursework and in public settings or formal situations.

Other varieties of language are often called **nonstandard**. Although these varieties may be restricted to a particular region or a particular ethnic group, most of us use some nonstandard language in our everyday speech and writing. Because of the lower prestige of nonstandard English, people who speak and write it may be wrongly labeled as unintelligent or uneducated. Standard English is not more logical or more inherently effective than the nonstandard varieties; it's just more acceptable to people, especially in formal writing.

Exercise 1.3

Using Standard English

Directions: Rewrite the following sentences in standard American English.

1. I knowed you wasn't from New Jersey.

   _____

2. Eddie and him drove home real slow.

   _____

3. We didn't do nothing but listen to records.

   _____

4. We thought you had drank all the ginger ale.

   _____

5. The children wanted to play by theirselves.

   _____

6. She don't take it serious because she don't believe in ghosts.

   _____

7. When they was in the planning stages, they underestimated the costs big-time.

   _____

8. I can't hardly believe what you said to the coach.

   _____

9. Sam and myself won't be going to the game.

   _____

10. The boss asked Derek if he had did his clean-up.

   _____

LANGUAGE CHANGE

For the most part, language changes because society changes. And while such change is inevitable, it is rarely predictable. Although some people see it as a sign of deterioration or decay, language change occurs so infrequently and so slowly that it seldom causes problems in communication or precision. Most change affects the lexicon (vocabulary) of a language: New words are added and others change meaning or acquire additional meanings. Changes in sentence structure are less frequent and take much longer to develop.

Exercise 1.4

Examining Changes in English

Directions: Translate these passages from Shakespeare's *Julius Caesar* into modern English and explain the grammatical changes you found it necessary to make.

1. Thou art a cobbler, art thou?

2. Wherefore rejoice? What conquests brings he home?

3. Dwell I but in the suburbs of your good pleasure?

4. O mighty Caesar, dost thou lie so low?

5. This was the most unkindest cut of all.

6. Think not, thou noble Roman, / That ever Brutus will go bound to Rome.

Exercise 1.5

Investigating Changes in Words

Directions: The meanings of words change, and the meaning a word once had may have little or no bearing on its meaning today. For example, the word *nice* used to mean "ignorant" or "foolish," but now it means "generally pleasing" or "carefully discerning." Check out the origins and history of the following terms in the *Oxford English Dictionary* or another book of word origins. What did the word used to mean? How has that meaning changed?

1. sail [*verb*]

2. drive [*verb*]

3. starve

4. meat

5. deer

6. villain

7. hussy

8. knave

9. lewd

10. knight

Chapter 2

Sentence Patterns

The exercises in this chapter will give you practice in recognizing and analyzing the basic sentence patterns and their parts. Before we examine the sentence as a whole, we will look at some of the basic components of sentences—words and phrases.

WORD CLASSES

Sentences are, of course, made up of words. Traditional grammarians classified these words into eight categories, called *the parts of speech,* in order to make their description of English conform to the word categories of Latin grammar. More recent grammarians, however, have looked closely at English and now classify words according to their form and their function in the sentence.

The four major classes of words in English are the *form-class words:* nouns, verbs, adjectives, and adverbs. These words provide the primary content in a sentence. Learning to identify form-class words will help you to understand how sentences are put together.

The key feature of form-class words is that they change form. They have endings (or spelling changes) that make specific grammatical distinctions.

Nouns

- have singular and plural forms: dog/dogs; woman/women.

- change form to show possession: the *dog's* owner; *women's* rights.

- are marked or signaled by articles (*a, an, the*) or other determiners: *a* dog, *that* woman, *my* pet, *some* people.

Verbs

- have present-tense and past-tense forms: bark/barked; buy/bought.

- have an *-s* form and an *-ing* form: barks/barking; buys/buying.

11

Adjectives

- have comparative and superlative forms: happy/happier/happiest; expensive/more expensive/most expensive.

- can be qualified by words like *very* and *too:* very happy, too expensive.

Adverbs

- have comparative and superlative forms: soon/sooner/soonest; carefully/more carefully/most carefully.

- can be qualified by words like *very* and *too:* very carefully, too soon.

- are often formed by adding *-ly* to adjectives: expensive ⟶ expensively; happy ⟶ happily.

We can distinguish adjectives from adverbs in three ways:

1. Most adjectives fit into both blanks of this "adjective test frame":

   The _____ NOUN is very _____.

   The *happy* wanderer is very *happy.*

   The *expensive* necklace is very *expensive.*

2. Adverbs are often movable:

   The dogs barked *frequently.*

   The dogs *frequently* barked.

   Frequently the dogs barked.

3. Adverbs can usually be identified by the information they provide: They tell *when, where, why, how,* and *how often.*

Exercise 2.1
Identifying Form-Class Words

A. *Directions:* Identify the form class of the underlined words in the following sentences as noun, verb, adjective, or adverb. Indicate the characteristics of form that you used to make your identification.

Example:

A ten-ton elephant <u>weighs</u> less than a <u>whale</u>.

weighs: verb—present tense, -s form; other forms would be weighed, weighing

whale: noun—marked by *a*; plural form would be whales

1. The sperm whale <u>stays</u> underwater for thirty <u>minutes</u> at a time.

2. Most whales <u>come</u> to the surface more <u>frequently</u>.

3. The <u>icy</u> waters of the Antarctic Ocean provide an abundant <u>supply</u> of plankton for these <u>huge</u> creatures.

4. A <u>small</u> <u>blue</u> whale eats as many as twenty-four <u>seals</u> every day.

5. These giant <u>mammals</u> <u>often</u> leap from the <u>water</u> just for fun.

6. Their tails <u>align</u> <u>horizontally</u> with their <u>bodies</u>.

B. *Directions:* Underline all the nouns, verbs, adjectives, and adverbs in the following sentences. Identify the class of each by writing one of these labels below the word: N, V, adj, or adv.

1. The young contestant seemed nervous.

2. The vapid host grinned foolishly.

3. Some raucous members of the audience laughed loudly at his silly comments.

4. The director often interrupts the program with trivial suggestions.

THE NOUN PHRASE

The most common word group in the sentence, one that fills many roles in the sentence patterns, is the **noun phrase** (NP), consisting of a noun **headword** together with its modifiers. As you may remember, the word *noun* is from the Latin word for "name"—and that's how nouns are traditionally defined: as the name of a person, place, thing, concept, event, and the like. But an even better way to recognize and understand nouns is to call on your language competence, to apply in a conscious way what you know intuitively about nouns. For example, one feature common to most nouns when we put them in sentences is the **determiner** that signals them:

<u>a</u> pizza

<u>the</u> game on Saturday

<u>every</u> class

<u>those</u> students standing on <u>the</u> corner

<u>several</u> friends from <u>my</u> hometown

<u>four</u> members of <u>our</u> speech team

<u>Tom's</u> friend

<u>that</u> problem

The articles *a* and *the*, demonstrative pronouns like *that* and *those*, possessive pronouns and possessive names like *my* and *our* and *Tom's*, indefinite pronouns like *several* and *every*, and numbers like *four*—all of these are determiners that signal the beginning of a noun phrase. Sometimes other words intervene between the determiner and the headword noun:

several <u>old</u> friends from my hometown

the <u>soccer</u> game on Saturday

a <u>delicious</u> pizza

that <u>recurring</u> problem

In each case, however, you can identify the headword of the noun phrase by asking *what?*

several what? (*friends*)

the what? (*game*)

a what? (a *pizza*)

that what? (*problem*)

When you become conscious of determiners, you'll begin to recognize how helpful they can be in discovering the opening of noun phrases.

We should note that there are several kinds of nouns that are not signaled by determiners. For example, proper nouns—the names of particular people, events, places, and the like (*Aunt Bess, President Lincoln, Mt. Rainier, Oklahoma, Main Street, Thanksgiving*)—rarely have determiners; abstract nouns (*happiness, justice*), mass, or noncountable, nouns (*homework, water*), and plural countable nouns (*people, children*) may also appear without them.

Another helpful way to recognize nouns—for example, to distinguish nouns from other word categories—is to recognize the various forms they have. Most nouns have both plural and possessive forms: *book, book's, books, books'; teacher, teacher's, teachers, teachers'; class, class's, classes, classes'*. If you can make a word plural, it's a noun: *two books, three classes, four teachers*. But even those that don't have a plural form, such as proper and abstract and mass nouns, generally do have a possessive form: *Joe's* book, the *water's* strange taste.

Exercise 2.2

Identifying Noun Phrases

Directions: Identify each noun phrase in the following sentences by circling the determiner and underlining the headword. Remember that some noun phrase slots will be filled by a single word—by a noun without a determiner or any modifiers.

Example:

(The) <u>bookstore</u> is holding (its) annual textbook <u>sale</u> on <u>Friday</u>.

1. My relatives have many odd habits.

2. Uncle Rondo has a morbid fear of aluminum cans.

3. His youngest daughter keeps her pet ocelot in the kitchen.

4. Our cousins from Arizona speak a secret language only on holidays.

5. Their father bought his second wife an antique cannon.

6. Aunt Helen's son plays the kazoo in a marching band.

7. My maternal grandmother dresses her three small dogs in sequined sweaters.

8. This eccentric behavior poses few problems for the neighbors.

9. Other people sometimes have trouble with these weird antics.

10. Some members of the family are not welcome everywhere.

THE PREPOSITIONAL PHRASE

The second kind of phrase we will examine is the prepositional phrase, a word group that shows up throughout the sentence, sometimes as a part of a noun phrase and sometimes as a modifier of the verb.

In the following list of noun phrases, the noun headword is shown in bold; the underlined word group that follows the headword in each case is a **prepositional phrase**:

>   several **students** <u>in my history class</u>

>   their **reports** <u>about the Civil War</u>

>   the **unit** <u>on the Civil War</u>

The prepositional phrase is one of our most common ways of modifying a noun, in order to add details or to make clear the identity of the noun:

>   that **house** <u>near the corner</u>

>   the **man** <u>with the camera</u>

>   a **ticket** <u>for the concert</u>

>   an **attorney** <u>from Florida</u>

There are, of course, many other forms of modifiers we could add to noun phrases:

>   that <u>white brick</u> **house** near the corner

>   the <u>tall</u> **man** with the camera <u>who just walked by</u>

For now we will concentrate on prepositional phrases. In the examples so far, we have seen the following **prepositions**: *in, about, on, near, with, for,* and *from.* In Chapter 12 of *Understanding English Grammar,* there is a list of about fifty more, all of which are among the most common words in the English language—words we use automatically every day.

The word group known as the prepositional phrase consists of a preposition and its object; the object is usually a noun phrase or a single noun, as the examples here show (*my history class, the Civil War, the corner, the camera, the concert, Florida*), but in later chapters you will see other word groups, such as verb phrases (gerunds), functioning as objects of prepositions. Chapter 12 also includes a list of phrasal prepositions, those that consist of more than one word. Among them are *according to, because of, except for, instead of, on account of,* and *in spite of.* It would be a good idea at this point to become familiar with all the possibilities.

When prepositional phrases modify nouns, they are functioning the way that adjectives do, so we call them **adjectivals**. When they modify verbs, they are functioning as adverbs do, so we call them **adverbials**. Like adverbs, they tell *when, where, how, why,* and *how often:*

My sister has developed some strange allergies <u>in recent years</u>.

<u>In the fall</u> my brother usually gets hay fever.

As you see, these adverbials are identical in form to the adjectival prepositional phrases: a preposition followed by a noun phrase. But the adverbial ones can be moved around in their sentences:

<u>In recent years</u> my sister has developed some strange allergies.

My brother usually gets hay fever <u>in the fall</u>.

That movability is an important difference between the two functions: The adjectival prepositional phrase cannot be moved from its position following the noun it modifies. Not every adverbial is movable either, but if a prepositional phrase can be moved, it is clearly adverbial.

Sometimes we use an adjectival prepositional phrase to identify or describe the object of another preposition:

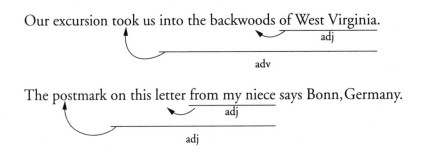

Exercise 2.3
Identifying Prepositional Phrases

Directions: Underline the prepositional phrases in the following sentences and identify them as adjectival or adverbial. (Note: Remember to call on your knowledge of pronouns in deciding if a prepositional phrase is part of a noun phrase. In the example, we could substitute *they* for the subject because it would replace "Many industries from the United States." When a prepositional phrase is part of a noun phrase, it is, by definition, adjectival.)

Example:

Many industries <u>from the United States</u> have built manufacturing
adj

plants <u>in Mexico</u> <u>in recent years</u>.
       adv   adv

1. The graduate assistant in our botany class gave a presentation about her bird-watching project.

2. Birdwatchers sighted an ivory-billed woodpecker for the first time in several decades.

3. The migration of birds is a fascinating subject.

4. Some North American birds fly to South America during their annual migration.

5. On Tuesday mornings the students from my study group take walking tours around the campus.

6. The person at the front desk is the receptionist for our department.

7. During the night our dog cornered a skunk behind the garage.

8. My allergy to dairy products causes problems for me in restaurants.

9. Quiz shows on television became popular again with many viewers.

10. Because of a mistake on my income tax return, the local IRS agent invited me to her office for an audit.

SENTENCE PATTERNS

The following exercises provide practice in recognizing and understanding **sentence patterns**—the focus of Chapter 2 in *Understanding English Grammar*. In these exercises you will be identifying slot boundaries and sentence patterns. Following are detailed steps that will lead you to the answers. Here's an example:

My roommates made a delicious meatloaf on Tuesday.

Step 1: Separate the subject and the predicate. The subject is the *who* or *what* that the sentence is about. In this example, it's *My roommates*. You can figure out that the subject noun phrase encompasses just those two words by substituting a pronoun:

<u>They</u> made a delicious meatloaf on Tuesday.

Don't forget, however, that sometimes an adverbial occupies the opening slot. You can identify adverbials by their movability. But in figuring out the sentence pattern, you should ignore them—they're optional.

Step 2: You'll recall that it's the predicate that determines the sentence pattern. First, of course, you must identify *made* as the predicating verb. One way to do that is to recognize *made* as an action—but that doesn't always work: Verbs are not always actions, and action words are not always verbs. In your study of verbs in Chapter 3 of *Understanding English Grammar* you'll discover that the predicating verb is the sentence slot that can have auxiliaries of various kinds. You can use that understanding to figure out that *made* is a verb by asking yourself, "Could I also say *has made* or *is making* or *might make*?" If the answer is *yes*, then you know that *made* is the predicating verb.

Step 3: How many slots follow the predicating verb? And what is the form of the word or word group that fills each slot? The word group following the verb *made* is a noun phrase, *a delicious meatloaf*. Here the opening article, *a*, is the clue: Words like *a* and *the* and *my*, the determiners, are noun signalers. When you see a determiner, you're at the beginning of a noun phrase (NP). And where does the NP end? You can prove that *on Tuesday* has its own slot by testing the boundaries of the meatloaf phrase: Substitute a pronoun:

My roommates made <u>it</u> on Tuesday.

Clearly, *on Tuesday* has its own slot: It's an adverbial telling *when*. (It's not an "on Tuesday meatloaf"!) You could also give it the movability test: It could just as easily—and grammatically—open the sentence.

On Tuesday my roommates made a delicious meatloaf.

Step 4. What is the sentence pattern? Because *a delicious meatloaf* and *my roommates* have different referents, the NPs in the formula have different numbers:

NP$_1$ Verb NP$_2$ (Adverbial)

And because *on Tuesday* is optional (the sentence is grammatical without it), you'll discover that the sentence pattern is VII.

Remember that the sentence patterns are differentiated by their verbs: *be*, linking, intransitive, and transitive. The four transitive patterns (VII to X) are subdivided on the basis of their verbs too. A verb with a meaning like "give" will have an indirect object as well as a direct object; and those two objects, you'll recall, have different referents:

Pattern VIII

The teacher gave <u>the students</u> <u>an assignment</u>.
             ind obj   **dir obj**

Some verbs will take both a direct object and an object complement—either an adjective (Pattern IX) or a noun phrase (Pattern X). In the case of Pattern X, the two NPs in the predicate have the same referent:

Pattern IX

The students consider <u>their teacher</u> <u>fair</u>.
                dir obj   **obj comp**

Pattern X

The students consider <u>their teacher</u> <u>a fair person</u>.
                dir obj   **obj comp**

(Reminder: A chart of the ten sentence patterns is displayed on the endpapers inside the book's cover.)

Exercise 2.4
Identifying and Diagramming the Sentence Patterns

Directions: Draw vertical lines to identify the slot boundaries in the following sentences; label each slot according to its form and function. In the parentheses following the sentence, identify its sentence pattern:

Example:

My roommates | made | a delicious meatloaf | on Tuesday. (<u>VII</u>)____

Form:	NP	V	NP	prep phr
Function:	subj	pred vb	dir obj	adv

Then, on separate paper, diagram the sentences. When you identify the sentence pattern, you establish the shape of the diagram. The main line of the diagram will look like the skeletal model for that pattern shown in Chapter 2 of *Understanding English Grammar.*

1. Rainfall originates in the ocean. (_____)

2. The evaporation of ocean water produces clouds. (_____)

3. The deepest part of the ocean is in the Marianas Trench. (_____)

4. Geologists consider the Dead Sea a lake. (_____)

5. The water in the Dead Sea is extremely salty. (_____)

6. Ocean currents flow counterclockwise in the Southern Hemisphere.

   (_____)

7. Angel Falls in Venezuela is the world's highest waterfall. (_____)

8. The pollution of rivers remains a major environmental problem throughout the world.
(_____)

9. Scientists discover many unusual creatures in the ocean's depths. (_____)

10. Irrigation gives desert regions a new lease on life. (_____)

LINKING VERBS

Patterns IV and V contain linking verbs other than *be*. *Be* is the most frequently used linking verb in English; it also has more forms and variations than other verbs. For these reasons, we have separated it from the other linking verbs to emphasize its special qualities.

Linking verbs connect the *subject* with a *subject complement*, a word or phrase that follows the verb and completes the meaning of the sentence. In Pattern IV, the subject complement is an adjective that describes or names an attribute of the subject. In Pattern V, the subject complement is a noun phrase that renames or identifies the subject—the NPs have the same referent.

A small number of verbs fit into these linking patterns. The common ones can be roughly divided into three categories:

- Verbs that express a change in state: *become, get, grow, turn*, etc.

- Verbs that express existence or appearance: *appear, seem, remain, stay*

- Verbs of perception: *look, feel, taste, smell, sound*

In addition to the limited number of common linking verbs, others not usually thought of as linking can, on occasion, be followed by an adjective and therefore fit into Pattern IV:

The screw *worked* loose.

The witness *stood* firm.

The well *ran* dry.

Very few verbs fit in Pattern V. The most common are *become* and *remain*; sometimes *seem, make, continue*, and *stay* will also take noun phrases as subject complements.

Most of the linking verbs listed here can also occur in other sentence patterns. You can often test for a linking verb by substituting a form of *be, seem*, or *become* in the sentence:

The screw *worked* loose = The screw *became* loose.

My uncle *remained* a bachelor = My uncle *was* a bachelor.

The meaning may change a little, but if the substitution produces a grammatical sentence, then you know you have a linking verb. Of course, the easiest way to recognize linking verbs is to identify the subject complement and understand its relationship to the subject.

Exercise 2.5

Identifying Linking Verbs and Other Patterns

Directions: Decide if the verbs in the following sentences are linking, intransitive, or transitive. Then write the sentence pattern number in the parentheses after each sentence.

1. Her face turned pale. (_____)

2. She turned her face to the sun. (_____)

3. You look sharp today. (_____)

4. The leaves on that tree turn bright red in the fall. (_____)

5. They stayed partners for many years. (_____)

6. We stayed at the Ramada Inn. (_____)

7. The governor stayed the execution. (_____)

8. My sister-in-law makes beautiful ceramic tiles. (_____)

9. Her ceramic tiles make great gifts. (_____)

10. This coffee tastes bitter. (_____)

11. The detective tasted traces of cyanide in the coffee. (_____)

12. The child fell sick during the night. (_____)

13. During thunderstorms my aunt always goes to the basement. (_____)

14. During thunderstorms our TV satellite goes haywire. (_____)

15. No snowflake falls in the wrong place. [Zen saying] (_____)

16. Men have become the tools of their tools. [Henry David Thoreau] (_____)

Exercise 2.6

Identifying More Sentence Patterns

Directions: Draw vertical lines to identify the slot boundaries in the following sentences; label each slot according to its form and function. In the parentheses following the sentence, identify its sentence pattern. Your instructor may want you to diagram these sentences on separate paper.

Example:

On its driest day, | the Susquehanna River | provides |
     prep phr   NP   V
      adv   subj   pred vb

one billion gallons of fresh water | to the Chesapeake Bay. (VII)
         NP   prep phr
      dir obj   adv

1. In the first few decades of the twentieth century, Sears sold houses through its catalogue.

   (_____)

2. Thousands of families in the Midwest still live in Sears houses. (_____)

3. In 1992 Sears announced the end of its catalogue sales. (_____)

4. In December the weather was warm and mild throughout the country.

   (_____)

5. Apparently our visitors from Reno missed their flight out of Chicago.

   (_____)

6. In grade school the Hardy Boys and Nancy Drew were my favorite fictional characters.

   (_____)

7. Adventure books gave me endless hours of pleasure during my childhood.

    (_____)

8. Yesterday my new car sputtered and stalled on the freeway during my morning com-

    mute to school. (_____)

9. The service station attendant simply ignored my pleas for help. (_____)

10. I consider such behavior a dereliction of duty. (_____)

PHRASAL VERBS

In your study of the sentence patterns you learned about the **particle**, a word that combines with a verb to form a **phrasal verb**. In the following example, *up* is a particle:

Pat looked up the word.

The phrasal verb *look up* has a distinctive meaning, one that is different from the combined meanings of *look* and *up*. In contrast, *up* is a preposition in this sentence:

Pat looked up the hall.

Here's a slot analysis of the two:

Pat | looked up | the word. (Pattern VII)

Form: N   vb   NP
Function: subj   pred vb   dir obj

Pat | looked | up the hall. (Pattern VI)

Form: N   vb   prep phr
Function: subj   pred vb   adv

And here is what they look like when diagrammed:

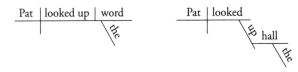

We could also say "Pat looked up," where *up* is an adverb:

Exercise 2.7

Identifying and Diagramming Phrasal Verbs

Directions: Draw vertical lines to show the slot boundaries in the following sentences, paying particular attention to the verbs. In the parentheses following the sentence, identify the number of the sentence pattern.

Example:

The police | are looking into | the suspect's activities. (__VII__) ____

(Helpful hint: One way to test a phrasal verb is to substitute a single word that means the same thing. Often you can find a synonym. In the previous example, we could substitute *investigating* for *looking into*.)

1. The office closes down on the weekends. (_____)

2. The horses galloped down the homestretch. (_____)

3. The wind blew down some trees. (_____)

4. The witness stood by her story. (_____)

5. The bailiff stood by the door. (_____)

6. The prosecutor suddenly stood up. (_____)

7. The defense wrapped up its case. (_____)

8. The jury carried out its duties in record time. (_____)

9. The judge threw out the verdict. (_____)

10. The reporters dashed out the door. (_____)

On separate paper diagram the ten sentences you just analyzed. Remember that all the words that make up the verb will be in the verb slot on the main line, as you saw in the diagram of "Pat looked up the word."

Test Exercise 2.8

Identifying Slot Boundaries and Sentence Patterns

Directions: Draw vertical lines to identify the slot boundaries in the following sentences; label each slot according to its form and function. In the parentheses following the sentence, identify its sentence pattern. [Answers are not given.]

Example:

My roommates | fixed | meatloaf and baked potatoes | for dinner | on Tuesday. (VII) ___
Form: NP   V   comp NP   prep ph   prep ph
Function: subj   pred vb   dir obj   adv   adv

1. Eager skiers crowded the slopes during the first snowfall of winter. (_____)

2. Uncle Ira built the neighbor children a tree house with real windows. (_____)

3. Sometimes our cat sits on their tree house for the entire day. (_____)

4. With further practice, Janet will become an excellent cellist. (_____)

5. My roommates and I broke down our expenses into four main categories.

    (_____)

6. Our biggest expense is the rent. (_____)

7. The rent for our apartment keeps us broke. (_____)

8. The rent for this apartment building makes our landlord a rich man. (_____)

9. My hands smell terrible because of these onions. (_____)

10. Lauren set up several interviews for next week. (_____)

11. Her present employer offered her a promotion and an increase in salary.
(_____)

12. The water in the middle of the river was swift and shallow. (_____)

13. The large trout were at the bottom of a deep pool. (_____)

14. Jeff reeled in a big one. (_____)

15. Then he threw it back. (_____)

16. My youngest brother is a very serious coffee drinker. (_____)

17. In spite of his coffee addiction, he sleeps soundly through the night.
(_____)

18. Coffee keeps many people awake. (_____)

19. The runner from Kenya stumbled and passed out at the finish line.
(_____)

20. The meet's officials declared him the winner of the marathon. (_____)

Chapter 3

Understanding Verbs

The formula you studied in Chapter 3 of *Understanding English Grammar*, known as the "verb-expansion rule," represents our system for generating all the possible grammatical verb forms. It explains our system for using auxiliaries:

VP = T (M) (have + -en) (be + -ing) MV

T stands for tense, either present or past. The tense is applied to the first word in the string:

pres + eat = eat(s)

past + eat = ate

present + have + -en + eat = have (has) eaten

past + have + -en + eat = had eaten

M stands for the modal auxiliaries, *can/could, will/would, shall/should, may/might, must, ought to:*

pres + can + eat = can eat

past + can + eat = could eat

pres + may + eat = may eat

past + will + eat = would eat

have + -en: This component of the rule says that when *have* serves as an auxiliary it is followed by the -en form (the past participle) of the main verb (or of the auxiliary *be*):

pres + have + -en + eat = have (has) eaten

past + have + -en + eat = had eaten

pres + have + -en + be + -ing + eat = has (have) been eating

past + have + -en + be + -ing + eat = had been eating

be + -ing: This component of the rule says that when *be* serves as an auxiliary, it is followed by the -ing form of the verb:

pres + be + -ing + eat = is (am, are) eating

past + be + -ing + eat = was (were) eating

past + may + be + -ing + eat = might be eating

MV, the main verb, will always be the last slot in the verb string. Its form will be determined by the auxiliary that precedes it or by **T** if there is no auxiliary:

pres + eat = eats

past + eat = ate

past + be + -ing + eat = was (were) eating

past + shall + eat = should eat

Exercise 3.1

Identifying Verb Strings

Directions: Underline the verb—along with any auxiliaries—in the following sentences. Then show the components of the verb-expansion rule that the verb string contains. Remember that in every case the first component is either present or past tense.

Example:

We <u>have finished</u> our homework.

pres + have + -en + finish _____

(Note that *have + -en* is not shown in parentheses here. The parentheses mean that the auxiliary is optional: We don't have to choose it. Here, however, we are examining what we did choose.)

1. Julie was feeling ill yesterday.

   _____

2. Our team has gone the extra mile.

   _____

3. The boss may give us a day off.

   _____

4. The police should have expected that problem.

   _____

5. My friends and I have been working hard on the political rally.

   _____

6. It could be a successful event for the candidate.

   _____

7. We had anticipated a big turnout.

_____

8. We know the problems.

_____

9. We can be there for dinner.

_____

10. I might have been thinking too optimistically.

_____

Exercise 3.2

Practicing with Verbs

Directions: Turn each of the following strings into a predicating verb; then use it in a sentence with "the students" as the subject.

Example:

    pres + will + be + -ing + work

    will be working / The students will be working on their projects this weekend.

1. pres + be + -ing + study

2. past + have + -en + study

3. past + be + -ing + be

4. past + can + have + -en + finish

5. pres + have + -en + be + -ing + help

   _____

   _____

6. past + shall + have + -en + win

   _____

   _____

7. past + be + -ing + work

   _____

   _____

8. pres + may + be + -ing + go

   _____

   _____

9. past + can + have + -en + be + -ing + make

   _____

   _____

10. past + have + -en + have

   _____

   _____

THE PASSIVE VOICE

The verb-expansion rule represents the system for generating verbs in all of the sentence patterns. You can think of it as the "active" rule. The four transitive-verb patterns, however, have another version: the **passive voice.** We go through two main steps in transforming an active sentence to passive:

1. The direct object of the active is shifted to subject position.

2. *be* + *-en* is added to the verb formula.

Here, for example, is an active sentence:

The students have eaten the pizza.

First, let's analyze the components of the verb, *have eaten:*

pres + **have** + **-en** + **eat**

To transform the sentence into the passive voice, we add *be* + *-en*, just before the main verb:

pres + **have** + **-en** + *be* + *-en* + **eat**

The passive verb becomes *has been eaten.*

You'll notice that when we shift the direct object, *the pizza*, into subject position, the sentence no longer has a direct object:

The pizza has been eaten.

We could add the original subject, or agent, to the passive by using a prepositional phrase (*by the students*), but often a passive sentence has no agent mentioned. The sentence is grammatical without it.

The resulting sentence,

may look like Pattern VI—but don't be fooled: It's still Pattern VII. Remember that sentences are classified into patterns according to their verbs. Pattern VI is the class of intransitive verbs. *Has been eaten* is clearly not an intransitive verb. How do you know? Because it's passive, and only transitive verbs have a passive version. (And how can you recognize it as passive? Because it has a form of *be* as an auxiliary *not* followed by an *-ing* verb.)

You can also identify the voice of the sentence—whether active or passive—on the basis of meaning. Is the subject the actor, or agent—the "doer" of the action named by the verb? Or is the subject the passive receiver of the action? Think about the pizza. It's not doing anything; something's being done to it!

The indirect object of a Pattern VIII sentence can also become the subject of the passive version:

> (active) The candidate granted <u>Tania</u> <u>an interview</u>.
>   ind obj   dir obj

> (passive) Tania was granted an interview.

Notice that the direct object (*an interview*) remains in its slot after the verb.

If the direct object of a Pattern VIII sentence is used for the passive subject, the indirect object (if retained) is usually expressed in a prepositional phrase beginning with *to* or *for:*

> An interview was granted to Tania.

Exercise 3.3
Transforming Active Sentences to Passive

Directions: In this exercise you will follow two steps in transforming the sentences into the passive voice:

Step 1: On the first line below the sentence, identify the components of the verb. Your answer will be in the form of a string, beginning with tense—present or past.

Step 2: On the remaining lines, write out the passive version of the sentence. Remember that the direct or indirect object will become the subject of the passive. Remember, too, that you will add *be* + *-en* to the components of the active verb. In some cases you may wish to include the active subject (as the object of the preposition *by*); in others you may wish to drop it.

Example:

> You <u>will retain</u> all of the components of the active verb string.
>
> pres + will + retain _____
>
> *Passive*: All of the components of the active verb string will be retained. _____

1. The mechanic has repaired my car.

    _____

    _____

2. He finally discovered the problem.

    _____

    _____

3. I should probably give the mechanic a tip.

    _____

    _____

4. All the candidates criticized the governor's tax program.

_____

_____

5. CBS is interviewing all of the candidates tonight.

_____

_____

6. Most of the networks will broadcast the president's economic address to Congress.

_____

_____

7. The network newscasters are calling the president's economic plan a failure.

_____

_____

8. Professor Arnold assigned the class extra homework for this weekend.

_____

_____

9. Professor Arnold could have given us a choice of several different term projects.

_____

_____

10. Someone has turned in my wallet to the lost-and-found.

_____

_____

CHANGING PASSIVE TO ACTIVE

To convert a passive sentence into an active one, begin by looking for these three elements:

1. *The agent or doer of the action expressed by the verb.* It's usually located in a *by* phrase. If an agent is not included in the passive sentence, then you'll have to create one. Remember, it serves as the subject of the active sentence.

2. *The* be *auxiliary in the passive verb.* It's always the last auxiliary in the verb string and is always followed by the *en* form of the main verb. You will delete this auxiliary and not include it in the active sentence.

3. *The subject of the passive sentence.* You will shift it to the object slot in the active sentence.

Let's take a look at a passive sentence and see how this analysis helps us to rewrite the sentence in active voice.

> **These lines were written by a famous poet.**

- The agent of the action is "a famous poet," which will become the subject of the active sentence.

- The passive auxiliary is "were," which is in the past tense. Delete it and change the main verb from "written" (the *-en* form) to "wrote" (the past tense).

- The passive subject is "These lines," which goes in the direct object slot of the active sentence.

> **A famous poet wrote these lines.** [*active version*]

Here are two more examples:

> **These lines are often quoted.**

- There's no agent, so supply a noun phrase like "people" as the subject.

- Delete "are" (present tense) and use "quote" (present tense) for the verb.

- Move "these lines" to the direct object slot. (Put the adverb "often" wherever it fits.)

People often quote these lines. [*active version*].

These lines have been frequently quoted by politicians.

- "Politicians" becomes the subject.

- Delete "been" but keep "have"; the main verb remains the *-en* form ("quoted").

- Use "these lines" for the direct object; put the adverb "frequently" before the main verb or at the end of the sentence.

    Politicians have frequently quoted these lines. [*active version*]

    Politicians have quoted these lines frequently. [*active version*]

With a "give" verb the passive subject may shift to the indirect object slot in the active version:

    The author was offered a huge advance for his new novel. [*passive version*]

    Several publishers offered the author a huge advance for his new novel. [*active version*]

Exercise 3.4

Changing Passive Sentences to Active

Directions: Change these passive sentences into active voice. Remember to locate the agent of the action, delete the passive *be*, and shift the passive subject to an object slot. If the agent of the action is not expressed in the passive sentence, you will have to supply a subject (such as *someone*) for the active sentence. Identify the sentence pattern of the active sentences that you produce.

Example:

> Many lives have been saved by the discovery of insulin.
>
> The discovery of insulin has saved many lives. (VII)

1. The indelible marker was invented by Sidney Rosenthal in 1952.

2. The Magic Marker was created for art and industrial uses.

3. More than half a billion markers are sold each year.

4. These markers have been used for branding cattle, camouflaging fishing lines, and marking up buildings and subway cars.

5. According to the National Graffiti Information Network, four billion dollars in damage to public property is caused annually by vandals.

6. The sale of Magic Markers to minors is being banned by some cities because of the graffiti problems.

7. Marker sales to minors were banned by the city of Lawrence, Massachusetts, in 1985.

8. A better solution to their graffiti problems should probably be found.

9. Magic markers are now being manufactured by Binney & Smith, Inc.

10. Crayola crayons have been made by that same company for many years.

Exercise 3.5
Changing the Voice of Sentences

Directions:

Step 1: In the parentheses after each sentence, identify the voice of the verb as active (A) or passive (P).

Step 2: Rewrite the sentences, changing the active ones to passive and the passive to active. Again, remember that the only difference between the passive and active verb strings is the presence or absence of *be* + *-en*.

Example:

Our company will give everyone a bonus at the end of the year. (ᴬ)

Everyone will be given a bonus at the end of the year. (ᴾ)

1. The employees in my department really appreciate their yearly bonus. (_____)

    _____

    _____

2. The company is also trying a new vacation plan. (_____)

    _____

    _____

3. Our company was awarded a big contract by the government. (_____)

    _____

    _____

4. Outside auditors recently gave our pension plan an excellent rating. (_____)

    _____

    _____

5. Our pension funds have been invested very wisely. (_____)

_____

_____

6. Our overtime hours could be cut back after Christmas. (_____)

_____

_____

7. My family considers me very lucky because of my good job. (_____)

_____

_____

8. Cuts in the overtime budget will eventually make the company stronger.

(_____)

_____

_____

9. A similar cut in extra pay should be taken by the CEO and the Vice President.

(_____)

_____

_____

10. Split work shifts might also be instituted. (_____)

_____

_____

Test Exercise 3.6

Identifying Sentence Patterns and Verb Components

Directions: In the parenthesis after each sentence, identify its sentence pattern. On the line below, show the components of the verb. Your instructor may also ask you to diagram the sentences and to transform those with transitive verbs into the passive voice. [Answers are not given.]

1. Very high cholesterol levels increase the risk of heart attacks. (_____)

    _____

2. According to recent research, very low levels may also be a health hazard.

    (_____)

    _____

3. Heart disease remains the major killer in this country. (_____)

    _____

4. The federal government has recently announced its new regulations for food labels. (

    _____)

    _____

5. Some manufacturers are already using the new format. (_____)

    _____

6. The old labels gave consumers very little information about fat content.

    (_____)

    _____

7. My doctor has always considered nutrition the key to good health. (_____)

_____

8. The whole family should be eating more fresh vegetables now. (_____)

_____

9. The family will be coming over for dinner on Saturday night. (_____)

_____

10. Because of my low-sodium diet, potato chips have been tasting extremely salty

   to me.(_____)

_____

Chapter 4

Sentence Transformations

The transformations you read about in Chapter 4 of *Understanding English Grammar* illustrate, perhaps better than any other example can, the intuitive, automatic nature of language. Rules about questions and other transformations are programmed into your subconscious from an early age. In the exercises here you will examine those transformations in a conscious way.

Exercise 4.1

Diagramming Questions

Directions: In the parentheses after each of the following questions, identify its sentence pattern. Then, on separate paper, diagram the question. Remember that the interrogative word always introduces the question, but in the diagram it will occupy the slot of the unknown information. (The yes/no questions are introduced by auxiliaries.)

Examples:

What have you done to your hair? (VII)

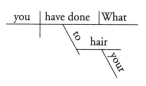

Have you ever hiked on Mt. Hood? (VI)

you | Have hiked
ever   *on* Mt. Hood

1. Where have you been hiding? (_____)

2. Shall we take the neighbor children with us? (_____)

3. Has the committee raised enough money for the party? (_____)

4. Has some money been stolen from the change box? (_____)

5. Is that your final answer? (_____)

6. Was Marie feeling better after her nap? (_____)

7. Which assignment should be done first? (_____)

8. Who created that computer virus? (_____)

9. When will Professor Watts give us back our essays? (_____)

10. Should all of us be there at the same time? (_____)

Exercise 4.2
Recognizing *There*

Directions: The purpose of this exercise is to help you distinguish the expletive *there* from the adverb *there*. Demonstrate the difference with a sentence diagram. Remember that the expletive *there* has no role in the underlying sentence; it is diagrammed on a separate line above the main clause. In the parenthesis, identify the sentence pattern.

Examples:

There's a piece of the puzzle missing. ($^{||}$)—

There it is, on the floor. ($^{|}$)—

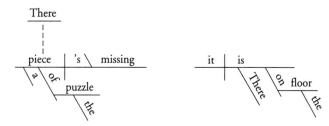

1. There's a strange dog barking in our backyard. (_____)

2. There we were in the middle of a snowstorm with no heat in the house.

    (_____)

3. There were several players seriously injured in Friday's game. (_____)

4. The ambulance was there within five minutes. (_____)

5. There was a doctor there within five seconds. (_____)

6. Hasn't there been a lot of rain this summer? (_____)

7. Lately there have been strange lights in the sky around midnight. (_____)

8. There's one now. (_____)

9. There will be beautiful decorations in the downtown area during December.

   (_____)

10. Is there nothing left of that huge pizza? (_____)

Exercise 4.3
Using the *It*-Cleft

Directions: Rewrite each of the following sentences with an *it*-cleft to vary the emphasis, according to the directions given. You may prefer to use the passive voice in some of your rewrites.

Example:

The New York Yankees won the World Series in 2000.

Emphasize the subject: It was the New York Yankees who won the World Series in 2000.

Emphasize the year: It was in 2000 that the New York Yankees won the World Series.

1. Negative political ads turned off a great many voters in the last election.

   Emphasize the subject: _____

   _____

2. Sir Humphrey Davy invented the carbon arc lamp seventy years before Edison's first light bulb.

   Emphasize the subject: _____

   _____

   Emphasize the time: _____

   _____

3. In November 1992, a fire in Windsor Castle caused over $100 million in damage.

   Emphasize the time: _____

   _____

Emphasize the subject: _____

_____

4. Several small boats capsized off Point Loma during a storm last week.

    Emphasize the where *adverbial:* _____

    _____

    Emphasize the when *adverbial:* _____

    _____

5. Many country music stars have built their own theaters in Branson, Missouri.

    Emphasize the place: _____

    _____

6. In 1998 breakthroughs in treatment brought new hope to people with AIDS.

    Emphasize the time: _____

    _____

    Emphasize the subject: _____

    _____

7. Ralph Nader's candidacy changed the presidential election of 2000.

    Emphasize the subject: _____

    _____

    Emphasize the direct object: _____

    _____

THE *WHAT*-CLEFT

A cleft transformation divides a sentence into two parts to give greater emphasis to one of the parts. *What*-cleft sentences put the emphasized part at the end. The first part becomes a clause introduced by *what*, and a form of the verb *be* links the two parts:

> I need a good night's sleep.

> <u>What I need</u> *is* a good night's sleep.

Sometimes the *what* shifts the entire verb phrase into the subject position, adding a form of *be* as the main verb:

> The poor voter turnout really surprised me.

> <u>What really surprised me</u> *was* the poor voter turnout.

Exercise 4.4
Using the *What*-Cleft

Directions: Use the *what*-cleft to emphasize one part of the following sentences.

Example:

> This version of the story illustrates the author's originality.

> <u>What this version of the story illustrates is the author's originality.</u>

1. Human error caused the explosion.

   _____

   _____

2. The goodness of strangers during the holidays always amazes me.

   _____

   _____

3. The poor condition of the lab equipment bothers me about chemistry class.

   _____

   _____

4. The magnificent display of fall colors brings tourists to New England in October.

   _____

   _____

5. You should ignore his sarcasm.

   _____

   _____

6. The voters want a fair election.

   _____

   _____

7. The enormous influence of lobbyists turns some people against politics.

   _____

   _____

8. My parents appreciate this school's easy-payment plan.

   _____

   _____

Test Exercise 4.5

Identifying Transformations

Directions: In the parentheses, identify the sentence pattern of the basic sentence underlying each of the following transformed sentences. On the line beneath the sentence, identify the transformation(s) that the sentence has undergone. You will find at least one example of each of the transformations you have studied: passive, interrogative, imperative, exclamatory, *do,* *there,* *it*-cleft, and *what*-cleft. Your instructor may also ask you to diagram the basic sentences. [Answers are not given.]

Example:

Have the students been given their homework assignment? (^{VII}) __

passive, interrogative _____

1. There is always a traffic jam in the parking lot at noon. (_____)

   _____

2. The street in front of our house was resurfaced on Monday. (_____)

   _____

3. Take a detour through the alley behind my house. (_____)

   _____

4. How scary the city sometimes seems at night. (_____)

   _____

5. How can our electronics industry compete with the Japanese? (_____)

   _____

6. Should our steel industry be given special subsidies? (_____)

   _____

7. There were too many suspects in last night's episode of *Law and Order.* (_____)

   _____

8. It was a jilted lover who gave McCoy the missing piece of evidence. (_____)

_____

9. What did you find enjoyable about that silly movie? (_____)

_____

10. What bothered me about that movie was its sophomoric humor. (_____)

_____

11. Is throwing cream pie in someone's face your idea of humor? (_____)

_____

12. Recall for me even one really funny line. (_____)

_____

13. Has the supervisor in your department always been considered a fair person?

(_____)

_____

14. Did you hear about the fight in the gym after the game? (_____)

_____

15. There were several students from our dorm being questioned by the police after

the fight. (_____)

_____

16. Don't make matters worse. (_____)

_____

Chapter 5

Modifiers of the Verb: Adverbials

Many of the sentences you have seen so far include **adverbials**—modifiers of the verb that add such information as time, place, reason, and manner. In Exercise 2.4 your task was to distinguish adverbial prepositional phrases from adjectivals, those that modify nouns. Here's the example from that exercise, with its three prepositional phrases:

> Many industries <u>from the United States</u> have built manufacturing plants <u>in Mexico</u> <u>in recent years</u>.

The first is adjectival, modifying *industries*. You can test its function by substituting a pronoun for the subject of the sentence:

> <u>They</u> have built manufacturing plants....

The fact that the pronoun substitutes for the entire phrase, "Many industries from the United States," demonstrates that the "from" phrase modifies the noun.

The "in" prepositional phrases, however, are clearly adverbial, telling *where* and *when* about the verb. The last one is easy to test: It could open the sentence without changing the meaning:

> In recent years they have built manufacturing plants in Mexico.

However, we probably wouldn't shift this particular "where" information:

> In Mexico in recent years, many industries have built manufacturing plants.

The sentence is grammatical, but it doesn't sound quite as natural.

The movability test is not infallible. There are a number of adverbs and adverbial prepositional phrases that would not be idiomatic in the opening slot. However, if the prepositional phrase *can* be moved to the opening, it is clearly adverbial.

Exercise 5.1
Recognizing Adverbials

Directions: This exercise is similar to the one you did in Chapter 2 where you distinguished adverbial and adjectival prepositional phrases. Here, too, the sentences include both functions of the prepositional phrase. They also include adverbs, some of which are recognizable by the *-ly* endings (adverbs of manner, you'll recall, are derived by adding *-ly* to adjectives). Others you can identify by the kind of information they contribute to the sentence.

Underline the adverbial words and phrases. Draw an arrow from the underline to the verb being modified.

Examples:

The people across the hall often have noisy parties on the weekends.

Several friends are coming to my apartment on Saturday night for a party.

1. In this part of the country, we often have exciting thunderstorms on summer evenings.

2. In California, people frequently have nightmares after an intense earthquake.

3. How do people in the far north live happily in winter with so few hours of daylight?

4. People often suffer severe depression during the dark days of winter.

5. According to recent estimates, almost 300 vertebrate species have become extinct during the past 300 years.

6. Nowadays extinctions occur because of human activity.

7. Several species are teetering precariously on the brink of extinction.

8. Many people work for years at very low wages.

9. A counter job at a fast-food restaurant will probably not make anyone rich.

10. During the last session of Congress, the lawmakers finally raised the minimum wage to a reasonable rate.

Exercise 5.2

Diagramming Practice with Adverbials

Directions: Using separate paper, diagram the following ten sentences from Exercise 5.1.

1. In this part of the country, we often have exciting thunderstorms on summer evenings.

2. In California, people frequently have nightmares after an intense earthquake.

3. How do people in the far north live happily in winter with so few hours of daylight?

4. People often suffer severe depression during the dark days of winter.

5. According to recent estimates, almost 300 vertebrate species have become extinct during the past 300 years.

6. Nowadays extinctions occur because of human activity.

7. Several species are teetering precariously on the brink of extinction.

8. Many people work for years at very low wages.

9. A counter job at a fast-food restaurant will probably not make anyone rich.

10. During the last session of Congress, the lawmakers finally raised the minimum wage to a reasonable rate.

Exercise 5.3
Identifying and Diagramming Adverbials

Directions: In this exercise, you will encounter all five forms of adverbials that you studied in Chapter 5 of *Understanding English Grammar:* adverbs, prepositional phrases, noun phrases, verb phrases, and clauses. Underline each adverbial and identify its form.

Example:

<u>Last night</u> the wind was blowing <u>hard</u>.
    NP   adv

Using separate paper, diagram the ten sentences. Remember that all of the words and word groups that you identified as adverbal will be attached to a verb.

1. At Mike's Halloween party, a ghostly face appeared in the window at midnight.

2. On Monday Sue stayed home to clean house.

3. My father moved to Florida last year when he retired.

4. I landed a part-time job in an art museum this summer.

5. Opportunities for full-time employment are limited in this economy.

6. A snowstorm blanketed the area very suddenly on Sunday night.

7. To get to work on Monday, I caught the early train.

8. To burn more calories when you walk, you can lengthen your stride.

9. When you take the stairs, your legs lift the entire weight of your body at every step.

10. To keep the fishing enthusiasts happy, the Fish Commission stocks the county's streams every spring.

Exercise 5.4

Combining Sentences

Directions: Combine each of the following pairs of sentences into a single sentence by reducing one of the original sentences to an adverbial clause. As you know, adverbial clauses begin with **subordinating conjunctions**, words that establish the relationship between clauses. Here is a list of the most frequently used subordinators:

To indicate time: before, after, as, as soon as, when, whenever, until, once

To indicate cause: because, since

To indicate purpose: in order that, so that

To indicate condition: if, provided that, once

To indicate place: where, wherever

To indicate concession: though, although, even though, except that

Put a comma after an adverbial clause that comes at the beginning of a sentence. When an adverbial clause follows an independent clause, no comma is needed, unless the subordinator expresses a contrast.

Examples:

Our family wanted to see Carlsbad Caverns.

We drove to New Mexico last summer.

We drove to New Mexico last summer because our family wanted to see

Carlsbad Caverns.

We arrived early in the morning.

We still had to wait an hour for a tour to begin.

Although we arrived early in the morning, we still had to wait an hour for

a tour to begin.

1. We waited for the tour to start.
   My sister and I read the brochure about stalactites and stalagmites.

   _____

   _____

2. These amazing formations look like artistic sculptures.
   They have been formed naturally by dripping groundwater.

   _____

   _____

3. We wanted to see these natural wonders with our own eyes.
   We would have to wait for the tour to start.

   _____

   _____

4. The tour finally started.
   It was certainly worth the wait.

   _____

   _____

5. We hiked along a trail more than 700 feet underground.
   We came to the largest subterranean chamber in the world.

   _____

   _____

6. We looked around the enormous room.
   We saw stalactites and stalagmites everywhere.

   _____

   _____

Exercise 5.5
Prepositional and Infinitive Phrases

Directions: The purpose of this exercise is to help you distinguish between prepositional phrases with *to* and adverbial infinitive phrases, which also begin with *to*. Underline each *to* phrase; identify each as *prepositional* (prep) or *infinitive* (inf); then give its function in the sentence. The infinitive phrases in this exercise will be adverbial (adv); the prepositional phrases will be either adjectival (adj) or adverbial (adv). Remember that the difference between the two kinds of *to* phrases is the form of the word group that follows: Infinitive phrases are verb phrases; a noun phrase will follow the preposition *to* as its object.

Example:

My roommate went <u>to the store</u> <u>to get some snacks</u>.
                      prep—adv   inf—adv

1. To keep the class happy, the teacher canceled Friday's quiz.

2. The road to freedom has always been stalked by death.

3. Jacqueline will go to graduate school to major in art history.

4. She will appeal to her parents to lend her the money for her first semester's tuition.

5. To get detailed directions to Bryce Canyon, Karl logged on to the Internet.

6. I wouldn't lend my car to him even if he paid me to use it.

7. The Sixth Amendment to the Constitution guarantees all citizens the right to a speedy and public trial.

8. Walter walked to the edge of the canyon and leaned over to get a better view.

9. To get on the waiting list for this class, students must submit their requests to the academic vice-president by noon tomorrow.

Exercise 5.6

Composing Adverbials

Directions: Finish these sentences, adding adverbials in the positions shown.

Example:

> [prep ph] the weather turned cold [adv].
>
> *Rewrite:* On Monday the weather turned cold suddenly. _____

1. [inf ph] the neighborhood children decided to start a lawn-mowing service [prep ph].

   _____

   _____

2. [prep ph] the children earned more money than they expected [clause].

   _____

   _____

3. [adv] [prep ph] the president announced a new economic plan [inf ph].

   _____

   _____

4. [clause] the Congress [adv] agreed that the new plan had merit.

   _____

   _____

5. [prep ph] the students were angry [clause].

   _____

   _____

6. [inf ph], Scott [adv] signed up for ballroom dancing.

_____

_____

7. The fans were ecstatic [NP] [clause].

_____

_____

8. Our relatives from Albuquerque arrived [adv] [prep ph].

_____

_____

9. [prep ph] my roommate lost his driver's license [clause].

_____

_____

10. [adv] I waited [prep ph] [inf ph] [clause].

_____

_____

Exercise 5.7
Composing Sentences with Adverbials

Directions: Follow the instructions for writing sentences that include adverbials. Remember that adverbial clauses and infinitives themselves contain verbs, so those two adverbial word groups can include other adverbials.

1. Write a sentence about one of your classes that includes an adverbial clause.

   _____

   _____

2. Write a sentence about a holiday that includes an adverb of manner. Underline the adverb.

   _____

   _____

3. Write a sentence about your plans for the future that includes two adverbial prepositional phrases. Underline them.

   _____

   _____

4. Write a sentence about your favorite sport that includes an adverbial noun phrase. Underline the adverbial.

   _____

   _____

5. Write a sentence about your neighborhood that includes both an adverbial infinitive and an adverbial clause. Underline and label the two adverbials.

   _____

   _____

6. Write a sentence about last weekend that includes both an adverbial prepositional phrase and an adjectival prepositional phrase. Underline and label the two.

_____

_____

7. Write a sentence about traveling that includes an adverbial prepositional phrase *within* another adverbial. Underline the prepositional phrase.

_____

_____

8. Write a sentence about summer that includes adverbials of three different forms. Underline the three and identify their forms.

_____

Test Exercise 5.8

Identifying Form and Function

Directions: Identify each of the underlined words and word groups according to both its form and function. *Form* refers to word categories (noun, verb, preposition, determiner, etc.), names of phrases (prepositional phrase, noun phrase, infinitive phrase), and clauses (adverbial clause). *Function* refers to the specific role the word or word group plays in the sentence: subject, direct object, modifier of *play*, etc. You'll find it helpful to picture the sentence on a diagram to figure out the function of the underlined element. [Answers are not given.]

Examples:	*Form*	*Function*
He drove the car <u>around the track</u>.	prep ph	modifier of "drove"
He drove the car around <u>the track</u>.	noun ph	obj of prep

1. They leave for Mexico <u>next Monday</u>. _____ _____

2. <u>Next Monday</u> is a holiday. _____ _____

3. We will go to the mall on <u>Monday</u>. _____ _____

4. Take this to the post office <u>before it closes</u>. _____ _____

5. Take this <u>to the post office</u> before it closes. _____ _____

6. We should send my aunt a card <u>this Christmas</u>. _____ _____

7. We should send <u>my aunt</u> a card this Christmas. _____ _____

8. She looked at me <u>as if I were crazy</u>. _____ _____

9. She looked at me as if I were <u>crazy</u>. _____ _____

10. <u>To find stamps for my collection,</u>
    I check the mail at the office. _____ _____

11. The mail <u>at the office</u> includes a lot
    of letters from overseas. _____ _____

12. <u>When</u> this semester is over, I'll be
    ready for a break from school. _____ _____

13. The president's plan for the economy
    drew <u>a lot of criticism</u>. _____ _____

14. Please come <u>in</u> and sit down. _____ _____

15. We turned <u>in</u> early last night. _____ _____

16. We turned in <u>early</u> last night. _____ _____

Chapter 6

Modifiers of the Noun: Adjectivals

The **noun phrase** is the most common word group in English, having many roles to play and many slots to fill in our sentences. In fact, the sentence you just read contains five:

the noun phrase   many slots to fill

the most common word group in English   our sentences

many roles to play

And if we include the proper noun *English,* as many linguists do when considering noun phrases, then we can count six.

   This chapter, which covers adjectivals, or noun modifiers, is actually about noun phrases. It describes the noun **headword**—the common element in all noun phrases—along with all of the modifiers that fill the slots before and after the headword.

THE DETERMINER

The opening slot of the noun phrase is filled by a **determiner**, the most common of which are the **articles**, *a(n)* and *the*. The possessives are another important group of determiners: **possessive pronouns** (*my, his, her, its, their, your*), **possessive nouns** (*Pam's*), and **possessive noun phrases** (*the neighbors'* yard, *my little sister's* bicycle). Two other classes of pronouns can also function as determiners: the **indefinite pronouns** (*several, many,* etc.) and the four demonstrative pronouns (*this, that, these,* and *those*). **Numbers** also act as determiners. The five determiners in the opening sentence of this chapter include two uses of the definite article (*the*), two uses of an indefinite pronoun (*many*), and a possessive pronoun (*our*).

   The determiner, then, signals the beginning of a noun phrase. In the first exercise you will review determiners and headwords. Next you will study the system of modifiers that fill the slots before and after the headword.

Exercise 6.1

Identifying Determiners and Noun Phrases

Directions. In the following sentences, circle the headword of each noun phrase; underline the determiner, if there is one, and label its word class.

Example:

The (bookstore) on the (corner) is holding its big (sale) this (week).
art   poss pro   dem pro

1. Several students in my math class have been absent since the midterm exam.

2. Our exams in that class would probably have challenged Einstein.

3. In my opinion, the professor's strict attendance policy causes nervous anxiety in many students.

4. Few substitute teachers in the public schools can serve a full year without any problems.

5. Many winners of this year's Grammy awards are absolute strangers to me.

6. I made these beautiful bouquets out of the flowers from our garden.

7. My brother's first wife now lives in Denver.

8. Their oldest son goes to his father's alma mater in Utah.

9. The basketball team made seven three-point shots in the first half of last night's game.

10. Our team will probably be invited to the NCAA tournament this season.

THE PREPOSITIONAL PHRASE

As you know from Chapter 5, one of the most common adverbial word groups is the prepositional phrase. It is also a common adjectival word group. Sometimes it's tricky to figure out which function a prepositional phrase is performing. For example, consider the following sentence:

They discussed their problem with the teacher.

Without more information, we don't know if the prepositional phrase modifies *discussed* or *problem.* In this case the sentence is ambiguous.

One important difference between the two functions is the movability of the adverbial and the nonmovability of the adjectival: An adjectival prepositional phrase is always there in the noun phrase, most of the time directly following the noun headword (sometimes in the subject complement slot). But most adverbial prepositional phrases are movable: Many can either begin or end the sentence without a change in meaning. For example, in this sentence,

We went to the Fiesta Bowl <u>on New Year's Day.</u>

the closing prepositional phrase could open the sentence with no change in meaning:

<u>On New Year's Day</u> we went to the Fiesta Bowl.

That movability indicates that the prepositional phrase is adverbial; it is not a modifier of *Fiesta Bowl.* In the case of adverbials, we also have meaning to help us. When the phrase tells *when,* as in our example, its purpose is clearly adverbial.

An adjectival phrase, however, will identify the noun it modifies, telling *which one.*

Their problem with the teacher is serious.

Which problem? The one with the teacher.

Exercise 6.2
Identifying and Diagramming Prepositional Phrases

Directions: Underline the prepositional phrases in the following sentences and identify them as either adjectival (adj) or adverbial (adv). In the parentheses after each sentence, identify the pattern of that sentence. Then, on separate paper, diagram the sentences.

Example:

My uncle <u>from Milwaukee</u> is moving <u>to Arizona</u> <u>for his health</u>. (VI)
          adj   adv   adv

1. The neighbors across the hall are having a party for the residents on our floor. (_____)

2. Some soccer teams in Europe have canceled their games with English teams because of the unruly fans. (_____)

3. Our art class was at the museum for three hours on Tuesday afternoon. (_____)

4. According to researchers, step aerobics provides an important workout for leg muscles. (_____)

5. High doses of Vitamin A can cause hair loss in some people. (_____)

6. Have you seen the beautiful flower gardens on our campus in the summer? (_____)

7. He found the old chair on his porch at a garage sale. (_____)

8. The new subway system in Los Angeles will eventually have an effect on the freeway traffic. (_____)

9. For eight months the teachers in the local school district have been working without a contract. (_____)

10. The candidates with the most money usually win by a comfortable margin. (_____)

THE ADJECTIVAL CLAUSE

The **adjectival,** or **relative, clause** occupies the last slot in the noun phrase. Often, of course, the clause is the only postheadword modifier; but in those sentences where there are others, the clause will be the last in line:

> The people in line who are buying tickets for the concert will probably have to wait for several hours.

As you learned in Chapter 6 of *Understanding English Grammar,* adjectival clauses are introduced by **relative pronouns** or **relative adverbs.** For the most part, those relatives are the same words that in Chapter 4 you learned to identify as interrogatives. When they introduce adjectival clauses, words such as *who* and *which* and *why* and *where* are not asking questions or suggesting them; they are relating a clause to a noun as a modifier:

> My biology professor, who does research on frogs, worries because some species are becoming extinct.

The relative pronoun renames the noun headword; that is, the noun being modified is the antecedent of the relative pronoun. In the preceding example, the antecedent of *who* is "my biology professor." Relative adverbs introduce clauses that modify certain kinds of nouns: *where* clauses modify nouns of place (such as *town*); *when* clauses modify nouns of time; *why* clauses modify the noun *reason.*

> The town where I was born goes to sleep at 8:00 P.M.

One of the most common of the relative clause introducers is the relative pronoun *that:*

> The flavor that I prefer is pistachio nut.

Relative pronouns always perform a grammatical function in the clauses they introduce. In the earlier *who* clause, *who* is the subject; in the *that* clause, *that* is the direct object. When *that* is the direct object in its clause, it may be dropped:

> The flavor I prefer is pistachio nut.

You can still recognize the clause because it has a subject and verb: *I prefer.*

PUNCTUATING ADJECTIVAL CLAUSES

The way an adjectival clause relates to the noun it modifies determines the punctuation. An adjectival clause that is not required for identifying, or defining, the noun is set off with commas:

> Hawthorne Road, which runs past our house, is being repaved.

> Julia Losa, who lives at the end of Hawthorne Road, won the lottery.

The clauses—*which runs past our house* and *who lives at the end of Hawthorne Road*—give extra information that is not needed to define Hawthorne Road or Julia Losa; they simply comment on the nouns they modify.

An adjectival clause that is needed to identify the noun it modifies is not set off with commas:

> The road that runs past our house is being repaved.

> The woman who lives at the end of Hawthorne Road won the lottery.

The clauses—*that runs past our house* and *who lives at the end of Hawthorne Road*—supply the information that is necessary to identify "the road" and "the woman." If these clauses were removed, the reader would no longer know which road is being repaved or which woman won the lottery. Such necessary clauses are written without commas.

Exercise 6.3

Identifying and Punctuating Adjectival Clauses

Directions: In the following sentences, underline the adjectival (relative) clauses. Put in commas if they are needed.

Example:

Margaret Mitchell, <u>who wrote *Gone with the Wind*</u>, was an Atlanta newspaper reporter.

1. Mitchell's novel which won the Pulitzer Prize in 1937 sold over twenty million copies in thirty languages and forty countries.

2. This historical novel which is written from a Southern point of view depicts the tumult and suffering caused by the American Civil War.

3. The heroine of the story is Scarlett O'Hara who is a willful, defiant, manipulative Southern belle.

4. Scarlett fancies herself in love with a man who does not acknowledge her love.

5. After the death of her second husband, Scarlett finally marries Rhett Butler who is more than a match for her fiery nature.

6. Scarlett longs for the day when her beloved family home will be restored to its former glory.

7. The movie that was made from the novel won ten Oscars and has become a classic.

8. The actress who played Scarlett in the movie was British.

9. Mitchell was born in Atlanta where she lived her entire life.

10. *Gone with the Wind* is the only novel she wrote.

THE PARTICIPIAL PHRASE

Another postheadword slot in the noun phrase is the **participial phrase**, an *-ing* or *-en* verb with all of its complements and modifiers. Unlike the adjectival prepositional phrase, the participial phrase is sometimes movable. We can think of the slot following the headword as the "home base" of the participial phrase, but when the participle modifies the subject, it can also open or close the sentence.

> The Boy Scouts, *carrying all their supplies on their backs,* finally reached their campsite on the mountaintop.

> *Carrying all their supplies on their backs,* the Boy Scouts finally reached their campsite on the mountaintop.

> The Boy Scouts finally reached their campsite on the mountaintop, *carrying all their supplies on their backs.*

The important feature to notice is that the noun being modified—in this case "Boy Scouts"—is the subject of the participle. A participle modifies its own subject. As you read in *Understanding English Grammar,* the participial phrase is, essentially, a reduced adjectival clause:

> The Boy Scouts, ~~who were~~ carrying all their supplies on their backs, finally....

We should note too that the diagram of the sentence always shows the participle attached to its subject as part of the noun phrase. In the case of this sentence, all three versions will be diagrammed the same:

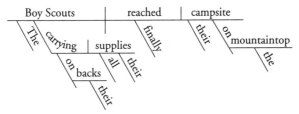

Note: In the case of the second version, the capital letter would be on "Carrying."

Exercise 6.4

Practicing with Participles

Directions: Rewrite each of the following pairs of sentences as a single sentence, turning one of the two predicates into a participial phrase. Items 9 and 10 have three sentences; turn two of them into participial phrases. Remember that you have a choice in placing the participle. And in some cases you also have a choice as to which sentence will be the main clause and which one the participle—as in the following:

Example:

> The sailboat glided across the bay.
> The sailboat looked majestic.
>
> *Rewrites:* The sailboat gliding across the bay looked majestic.
>
> > or
>
> Looking majestic, the sailboat glided across the bay.

(Note: In some cases you may have to change the auxiliaries.)

1. Satellites circle the earth.

    Satellites take useful pictures for weather predictions.

    _____

2. Ms. Ruggles was angered by the impertinence of the headwaiter.
    Ms. Ruggles turned and stalked out of the restaurant.

    _____

    _____

3. The shortstop leaped high in the air.
    The shortstop speared the line drive that would have won the game.

    _____

    _____

4. I have made the apartment quite cheerful looking.
   I have painted the living room blue and white.

   _____

   _____

5. My mother is a teacher.
   My mother has a long holiday at Christmas.

   _____

   _____

6. A man was standing in the hotel window.
   Nobody could identify the man.

   _____

   _____

7. The two boys were fascinated by the skills of the weaver.
   The two boys sat and watched the weaver's flying fingers for hours.

   _____

   _____

8. The fans crowded into the arena.
   The fans were hoping for a league championship.

   _____

   _____

9. Jean squinted hard at the note.
   Jean read the note in the dim light.
   The light came through the dirty window.

   _____

   _____

   _____

10. The passengers were seated in the back of the bus.
    They could not see the door.
    The deer were running across the road.

    _____

    _____

    _____

Exercise 6.5

Identifying and Diagramming Postnoun Modifiers

Directions: Underline all the postnoun modifiers in the following sentences. Label their form by writing one of these abbreviations below them: prep ph (for adjectival prepositional phrases), part ph (for participial phrases), and adj cl (for adjectival clauses).

Example:

The teenager <u>who lives across the street</u> rakes the leaves <u>in our yard </u>for a
                       adj cl   prep ph
reasonable price.

1. Marcus knows that man who is waving to us.

2. The man waving to us works at the fish market on Broadway.

3. Our music teacher, who is a veteran of the Vietnam War, visited the VietnamMemorial in Washington during spring break.

4. The Memorial is a place where the veterans who go there can honor their comrades.

5. The lumber industry in the Pacific Northwest, which always fluctuates with the economy, was a victim of the recession that occurred in the late 1980s.

6. Where did you put the groceries we bought for our trip?

7. My father, who hates yard work, paid the man mowing the lawn an extra bonus.

8. The students lined up in the gym are purchasing tickets for the big gymnastics meet on Friday.

9. The town where I was born is known for its beautiful iris gardens.

10. On the day when they announced the winners of the ice-sculpture contest, our sorority, which won first prize, skipped classes to celebrate.

11. The applicants complaining loudest are the ones with the weakest credentials.

12. He has all the virtues I dislike and none of the vices I admire.
    [Winston Churchill]

Now diagram these sentences on separate paper. In preparation for that job, draw lines to show the boundaries of the sentence slots and identify the sentence patterns.

Exercise 6.6

Composing and Using Noun Phrases

Directions: Generate noun phrases that conform to the following patterns; then for each NP write a sentence in which you use it as directed.

Example:

> det + adj + N + prep phrase (use as object of a preposition)
>
> my new friend from Des Moines
>
> I talked to my new friend from Des Moines.

1. det + n + N + prep phrase (use as subject)

   _____

   _____

2. det + adj + N + part phrase (use as direct object)

   _____

   _____

3. det + N + part phrase (use as subject complement)

   _____

   _____

4. det + N + part phrase + clause (use as subject)

   _____

   _____

5. det + adj + N + clause (use as indirect object)

_____

_____

6. det + adj + n + N (use as direct object)

_____

_____

7. det + N + part phrase (use as object of preposition)

_____

_____

8. det + N + clause (use as object complement)

_____

_____

9. det + past + N + prep phrase (use as subject complement)

_____

_____

Exercise 6.7
Revising Adjectival Clauses

Directions: The following sentences include adjectival clauses as modifiers in some of the noun phrases. Revise the sentences by reducing the adjectival clauses to verb phrases (participial phrases), prepositional phrases, noun phrases, or adjective phrases—if you can do so without losing information. Write your answers on the lines provided or on separate paper.

Example:

My neighbor *who lives across the street* raked my yard last week.

Rewrite: My neighbor across the street raked my yard last week.

1. San Antonio, Texas, which lies halfway between the east and west coasts, is the tenth largest city in the U.S.

   _____

   _____

2. The trees that were covered with mistletoe were half dead.

   _____

   _____

3. The theory of relativity, which Einstein developed, was presented to the scientific world in an article that was published in 1905.

   _____

   _____

4. According to some people, the Loch Ness monster, who is known as Nessie, may have some relatives who live in the lakes and coastal waters of British Columbia.

   _____

   _____

5. The International Date Line is an imaginary line that is fixed at 180° longitude, which is the location on earth that is exactly opposite Greenwich, England.

   _____

   _____

6. People who are interested in becoming astronauts should study science or engineering when they are in college.

   _____

   _____

7. According to researchers who work at the Boston University School of Medicine, men who are bald have an increased risk of heart attack.

   _____

   _____

8. The statistics that were reported on baldness do not apply to men who have receding hairlines.

   _____

   _____

9. People who are worried about preservatives should not be concerned about the preservatives that are added to bread to keep it fresh longer.

   _____

   _____

10. Children who are left-handed have more accidents than those who are right-handed, according to pediatricians who conducted a study at the Arkansas Children's Hospital.

   _____

   _____

DANGLING MODIFIERS

As you learned in Chapter 7 of *Understanding English Grammar,* readers assume that introductory participial and infinitive phrases will have the same subject as the subject of the main sentence. If that is not the case, the modifier "dangles":

> Staring in disbelief, the car jumped the curb and crashed into a mailbox.
>
> [Who was staring? Not the car.]
>
> To maintain a C average, a tutor meets with Tiffany three times a week.
>
> [Tiffany, not the tutor, wants a C average.]

You can usually revise dangling modifiers in one of two ways, depending on what you want to emphasize in the sentence:

- Make the subject of the main clause the same as the subject of the participle or infinitive:

  > Staring in disbelief, I watched the car jump the curb and crash into a mailbox.
  > To maintain a C average, Tiffany meets with a tutor three times a week.

- Rewrite the dangling modifier as a clause with its own subject and verb:

  > As I stared in disbelief, the car jumped the curb and crashed into a mailbox.
  > Because Tiffany wants to maintain a C average, her tutor has to meet with her three times a week.

Exercise 6.8
Revising Dangling Modifiers

Directions: Rewrite the following sentences to eliminate any dangling modifiers. Some sentences can be revised in more than one way.

1. Wearing her mother's wedding gown, Tanya's father walked her down the aisle.

2. Walking around the museum, the exquisite statues on display are my favorites of all the exhibits.

3. To understand the causes and to find a cure, arthritis is being studied extensively in medical laboratories throughout the country.

4. When only six years old, Brad's parents quit their jobs and joined a commune in Idaho.

5. Stalled at the railroad crossing, the train, rushing toward the car on the tracks, slowed down just in time to avoid a collision.

6. While jogging on a narrow country road, a pickup truck, driving erratically, forced me off the road and into the ditch.

7. Outdated and completely unworkable, a joint committee of administrators, faculty, and student leaders has been charged with revising the current Dormitory Visitation Policy.

8. To finish her term paper by the mid-semester deadline, it was clear to Angela that she would need a lot of time in the library.

9. Tracking further west than anticipated, forecasters at the National Storm Center say Hurricane Ivan will reach the Florida coast by nine p.m.

10. Excited by the pounding music, there was nothing to do but join the crowd on the dance floor.

MODIFIER PLACEMENT

You can ensure the correct interpretation of your sentences by paying close attention to where you place your modifiers. Consider how the meaning changes in these two sentences when the adverbial NP is shifted to a different position:

<u>Several times</u> the teacher told us to proofread our papers.

The teacher told us to proofread our papers <u>several times</u>.

A carelessly placed modifier can badly skew the meaning of a sentence:

DARE is sponsoring a series on drugs for local college students.

DARE is not in the business of acquainting college students with drugs to use. The meaning is clearer this way:

DARE is sponsoring a series for local college students on the dangers of drug use.

Putting the adjectival phrase next to the noun *series* illustrates the general rule about where to place a modifier: **as close as possible to the word it modifies.**

Exercise 6.9
Revising Misplaced Modifiers

Directions: Rewrite the following sentences to eliminate problems with modifier placement.

1. You are welcome to visit the cemetery where famous Russian artists and writers are buried daily except Thursday.

2. Otis was robbed at gunpoint in the elevator where he lives.

3. The cause of death was determined to be strangulation by the medical examiner.

4. Our company makes real wooden furniture for cats with removable parts.

5. The Diamondbacks' starter was facing a batter who can knock any pitch he can reach over the fence.

6. The mother of the accused killer said God would judge her son in a news conference on Friday.

7. Already legally blind, the doctors told her recently that her sight would soon be gone.

8. We are especially appealing to those who do not usually attend fund-raising events.

9. Jewel may be the first folksinger to take the stage with her guitar in four-inch heels and a miniskirt.

10. Mrs. Fisher's dog follows her car to the restaurant where she works and sleeps under the automobile all day.

Test Exercise 6.10
Form and Function

Directions: On the lines following the passage, identify each of the underlined elements according to both its form and its function. Remember that *form* refers to word categories (noun, verb, preposition, etc.), names of phrases (prepositional phrase, noun phrase, infinitive phrase, participial phrase, etc.), and clauses (adverbial clause, adjectival [relative]clause). *Function* refers to the specific role the word or word group plays in the sentence: subject, direct object, modifier of *play*, etc. You'll find it helpful to picture the sentence on a diagram to figure out the function of the underlined item. [Answers are not given.]

The Navajo Code Talkers took part in every assault <u>that the U. S. Marines conducted</u>
1

<u>in World War II</u>. They transmitted messages <u>by telephone and radio</u> in their native
2

language—a code <u>the Japanese never broke</u>.
3

Navajo answered the military requirement for an undecipherable code <u>because it</u>

<u>had never been written down</u>, <u>making it unintelligible without Navajo help</u>. In 1942,
4   5

twenty-nine Navajos were recruited <u>to create the code</u>. They developed a dictionary of
6

words <u>for military terms</u>, <u>which they memorized during training</u>. <u>When a Code Talker</u>
7   8   9

completed training, he was sent to a Marine unit <u>deployed in the Pacific theater</u>. The
10

original group became <u>an elite corps of 425 Navajo Code Talkers</u>. Navajo remained
11

potentially <u>valuable</u> even after the war. In 1968 America <u>finally</u> learned of the
12   13

extraordinary contribution <u>that a handful of Native Americans had made to the war effort</u>.
14

    Form   Function

1. _____   _____

2. _____   _____

3. _____   _____

4. _____   _____

5. _____   _____

6. _____   _____

7. _____   _____

8. _____   _____

9. _____   _____

10. _____   _____

11. _____   _____

12. _____   _____

13. _____   _____

14. _____   _____

Chapter 7

The Noun Phrase Slots: Nominals

In Chapter 7 of *Understanding English Grammar* you learned the word **nominal**, the term that refers to the functions that noun phrases carry out. As you know, there are many specific nominal functions: Subject, subject complement, direct object, indirect object, and object complement are the NP slots in the sentence-pattern formulas. Another common nominal function is that of object of the preposition. The word *nominal,* then, is the general term for the function; these other words—subject, direct object, and so on—name the specific nominal functions. Another of those specific functions is the **appositive**, a structure—generally a noun phrase—that adds information by renaming another nominal.

APPOSITIVES

The **appositive**, which is usually a noun phrase in form, can be thought of as nominal and adjectival. It has features of both: It renames another noun phrase or other nominal and can often substitute for that nominal; as part of an NP, it adds information as adjectivals do.

> My large car, <u>an eight-cylinder model</u>, uses a lot of gas.

> My sister's car, <u>a Japanese import</u>, is inexpensive to drive.

Here the appositives give more details about the noun *car;* they can also replace the nouns they modify:

> <u>An eight-cylinder model</u> uses a lot of gas.

> <u>A Japanese import</u> is inexpensive to drive.

Sometimes the appositive that modifies the subject can be placed at the beginning of a sentence:

> <u>A Japanese import</u>, my sister's car is inexpensive to drive.

Exercise 7.1
Using Appositives

Directions: In this exercise you will practice adding appositives to one of the noun phrase slots by combining sentences. In each of the following sets of sentences, the second adds a detail about one of the noun phrases in the first. Your job is to turn that detail into an appositive. Write your answers on the lines provided or on separate paper.

Example:

Aunt Rachel loves her job. She's a butcher at Safeway.

Rewrite: Aunt Rachel, a butcher at Safeway, loves her job.

[Note that in Sentence 10 there are two details to turn into appositives.]

1. I have heard that the crew cut is coming back in style. That haircut was the hallmark of the 1950s.

   _____

   _____

2. In the spring, many of Pennsylvania's wooded areas are filled with mountain laurel. Mountain laurel is the official state flower.

   _____

   _____

3. The deepest part of the ocean is located in the Western Pacific near the island of Guam. It is the Marianas Trench.

   _____

   _____

4. I grew up in Silverton, Oregon. It's a small town in the Willamette Valley.

   _____

   _____

5. The paper nautilus octopus lives in the coastal waters of Japan. This species of octopus is a rare marine animal.

_____

_____

6. In 1991 scientists identified a new species of whale. The new species is the pygmy beaked whale.

_____

_____

7. My sister's birthday sometimes falls on Mother's Day. Her birthday is May 11.

_____

_____

8. Kodak employs 40,000 people. It is the largest employer in Rochester, New York.

_____

_____

9. During its annual migration, the golden plover flies from the Arctic to Argentina. This bird is an amazing navigator.

_____

_____

10. My cousin just got a summer job at Graceland. He's a student at the University of Memphis. Graceland is Elvis Presley's estate.

_____

_____

FORMS OF NOMINALS

The most common unit, or form, that functions as a nominal, as you know, is the noun phrase. Except for a few pronouns, all of the nominals in Exercise 7.1 are nouns or noun phrases. However, in Chapter 7 of *Understanding English Grammar* you saw that other forms—verb phrases and clauses—can fill the nominal slots:

> <u>Riding a bicycle</u> is terrific exercise.

> Mike is planning <u>to buy a new bike</u>.

> I wonder <u>who owns this mountain bike</u>.

In the first example an *-ing* verb phrase, a gerund phrase, fills the subject slot; in the second an infinitive phrase occupies the direct object position; and in the third a nominal clause is the direct object.

NOMINAL VERB PHRASES

Nominal verb phrases come in two forms, the gerund and the infinitive, as illustrated by the earlier examples:

> <u>Riding a bike</u> is terrific exercise. [gerund]

> Mike is planning <u>to buy a new bike</u>. [infinitive]

The diagrams will help you recognize both of the verb phrases—*riding a bike* and *to buy a new bike*—as Pattern VII:

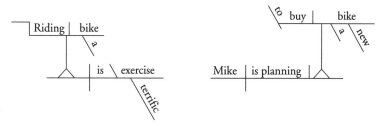

We frequently use gerund phrases and infinitive phrases to fill the subject or direct object slots in sentences:

subject: <u>Missing that turn on the highway</u> has made us late.

                 <u>To get home by midnight</u> will now be impossible.

direct object: I wanted <u>to lose thirty pounds</u>.

I tried <u>skipping every other meal</u>.

But we can also use these verb phrases in other nominal slots:

subject complement: Our toughest job is <u>finding qualified candidates</u>.

Our plan is <u>to advertise in the school newspaper</u>.

object of a preposition: He cannot discipline the children without <u>losing his temper</u>.

Exercise 7.2

Understanding Nominal Verb Phrases

Directions: This exercise has two steps:

Step 1: Reduce the predicate in each of the following sentences into (1) an *-ing* phrase and (2) an infinitive phrase.

Example:

We mowed the lawn for the neighbors.

-ing: mowing the lawn for the neighbors

infinitive: to mow the lawn for the neighbors

1. Our candidate won the election in a landslide.

2. We went to the movies.

3. Shelley lost her keys.

4. Terry is a good teacher.

5. I made too many mistakes on this biology homework.

_____

_____

6. Stacie painted her bedroom lavender.

_____

_____

7. The instructor gave the students an extra assignment.

_____

_____

8. Pat felt upset about the homework.

_____

_____

Step 2: Write eight sentences, including as a nominal either the *-ing* phrase or the infinitive phase you wrote in Step 1.

Example:

We decided to mow the lawn for the neighbors.
_____

or

Mowing the lawn for the neighbors was a good idea.
_____

1. _____

_____

2. _____

   _____

3. _____

   _____

4. _____

   _____

5. _____

   _____

6. _____

   _____

7. _____

   _____

8. _____

   _____

Exercise 7.3

Understanding *To*-Phrases

Directions: You may recall Exercise 5.6, where you distinguished the prepositional phrase with *to* from the adverbial infinitive phrase. The discussion of nominals in Chapter 7 of *Understanding English Grammar* introduced you to the nominal functions of the infinitive. So in this exercise you will find prepositional phrases, nominal infinitives, and adverbial infinitives—all introduced by *to*. One helpful way to distinguish the adverbial infinitive is by its underlying meaning: In nearly every case it answers the question *why;* and it can be expanded with *in order: I went home to study* = *I went home in order to study.* And of course the nominal infinitive occupies a noun phrase slot in the sentence pattern.

Underline each *to*-phrase in the following sentences and label each as pp (prepositional phrase), nom (nominal infinitive), or adv (adverbial infinitive). Your instructor may also ask you to diagram these sentences.

Example:

We went <u>to the computer show</u> <u>to check out the new war games</u>.
               PP   adv

1. To keep the class happy, the teacher canceled Friday's quiz.

2. To my way of thinking, to make the Dean's List is an accomplishment.

3. I am hoping to graduate at the end of the summer.

4. I will appeal to my parents to pay for my summer tuition.

5. To get a good job with a decent salary, you need to have experience.

6. To get experience you first need to be hired.

7. People go to great lengths to find that perfect job.

8. What I am planning to do after graduation will be a shock to my parents.

9. I have decided to go to graduate school to major in art history.

10. I think that I would like to work in an art museum.

NOMINAL CLAUSES

Clauses that occupy nominal slots have all the qualities of sentence patterns: a subject, a predicating verb, and any required slots following the verb, as well as optional elements. The only difference between these clauses and the sentences we have studied so far is that these are not independent clauses: They are part of another sentence. But, like sentences, they can also be classified according to their sentence patterns.

Nominal clauses are introduced by two kinds of words: **interrogatives** and **expletives**. In the mountain bike example, the clause is introduced by the interrogative *who*, which fills the subject slot in its own clause:

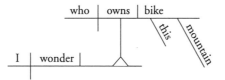

The interrogative always plays a role in the clause it introduces, but no matter what that role is, the interrogative introduces the clause:

I wonder <u>what brand this bike is</u>.

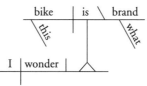

Nominal clauses are also introduced by the expletives *that, if, whether,* and *whether or not.* One important difference between the two kinds of introducers is that the expletive plays no part in its own clause, as the following diagram shows:

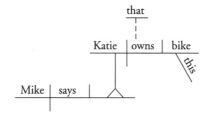

Exercise 7.4

Identifying and Diagramming Nominal Clauses

Directions: Each of the following sentences includes a clause in a nominal position. Underline the clause; identify its function in the sentence; then identify the pattern of the nominal clause. On separate paper, diagram the sentences in this exercise.

Example:

Do you know <u>where the children are</u>?

direct object—Pattern I _____

(Note that while this nominal clause is Pattern I, the main clause is Pattern VII.)

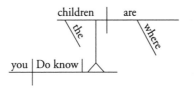

1. Where you spend your time is your own business.

    _____

2. I understand that Joe was fired from his new job.

    _____

3. Joe's problem is that he's not very efficient.

    _____

4. Joe thinks that the boss should have given him a raise.

    _____

5. You decide which movie we should rent.

    _____

6. I can't remember when I last rode on the subway.

_____

7. Why you look so sad is a mystery to me.

_____

8. I don't know if I can pass this course.

_____

9. How I could have done so badly on the midterm simply escapes me.

_____

10. The problem with this soup is that I made it too salty.

_____

Exercise 7.5
Identifying Dependent Clauses

Directions: You have studied three different kinds of dependent clauses—adverbial clauses, adjectival (or relative) clauses, and nominal clauses. The three are introduced by different kinds of words—adverbial clauses by subordinating conjunctions, adjectival clauses by relative pronouns and relative adverbs, and nominal clauses by expletives and interrogatives. And of course the three kinds of clauses function differently in their sentences: Adverbial clauses modify verbs; adjectival clauses modify nouns; and nominal clauses fill NP slots as subjects, direct objects, and so on. Underline the dependent clauses in the following sentences. Identify each as adverbial (adv), adjectival (adj), or nominal (nom); then give its specific function in the sentence. (If adverbial, what verb does it modify? If adjectival, what noun does it modify? If nominal, what NP slot does it fill?)

<u>Even before the fire alarm sounded</u>, I sensed <u>that something was happening</u>.
     adv—mod. *sensed*   nom—dir obj

1. I smelled smoke before I heard the fire alarm.

2. The pathologist could not state the exact time when death had occurred.

3. The tragedy of life is that people don't change. [Agatha Christie]

4. If you tell us your phobias, we will tell you what you are afraid of.

   [Robert Benchley]

5. The trouble with being in the rat race is that even if you win you're still

   a rat. [Lily Tomlin]

6. Experience is the name that everyone gives to their mistakes. [Oscar Wilde]

7. When you don't know where you are going, any road will take you there.

8. The attorney Brenda hired asked her if she had read the contract before she signed it.

9. Those who write clearly have readers; those who write obscurely have commentators. [Albert Camus]

10. A bore is a person who talks when you want him to listen. [Ambrose Bierce]

11. For those who like that sort of thing it is the sort of thing they like. [Muriel Spark]

12. Conscience is the inner voice that warns us somebody may be looking. [H. L. Mencken]

Your instructor may ask you to diagram these sentences on separate paper.

Exercise 7.6

Nominals and Sentence Patterns

Directions: (1) In the parentheses identify the sentence pattern of the main clause; (2) underline any nominal clauses or nominal verb phrases; (3) on the line below the sentence name the function of each underlined clause or phrase and identify its sentence pattern.

Example:

I hope <u>that the rain stops soon</u>. (VII)

direct object—Pattern VI

1. Collecting stamps is my hobby. (_____)

   _____

2. How you spend your allowance is your own business. (_____)

   _____

3. I am planning to give my dad a necktie for his birthday. (_____)

   _____

4. Elena's career goal is to become a doctor. (_____)

   _____

5. Elena's mother thought she wanted to go to nursing school. (_____)

   _____

6. The hikers decided to rest for a few minutes. (_____)

   _____

7. Painting the kitchen cupboards green was a big mistake. (_____)

   _____

8. Everyone on my floor loves watching college basketball on television. (_____)

   _____

9. We are wondering which teams will reach the final four. (_____)

   _____

10. Everyone knows that going to college is expensive. (_____)

   _____

Using separate paper, diagram the ten sentences in this exercise. Remember that you have already done a great deal of the analysis for those diagrams: You have identified the sentence pattern of each main clause as well as both the sentence pattern and the function of each embedded clause and verb phrase. With that information you know what the skeletal diagram will look like.

Example:

   I hope that the rain stops soon.

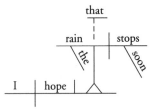

Exercise 7.7

Identifying Nominal Form and Function

Directions: The underlined elements in the following paragraph are nominal in function. On the lines following the passage identify, first, the *form* of each and, second, its *specific function*. *Form* includes such labels as noun, noun phrase, infinitive phrase, gerund phrase, and clause; *function* refers to the sentence slots—subject, direct object, object of preposition, etc. You'll find it helpful to picture the sentence on a diagram.

<u>My son</u> was always <u>an avid collector</u> in his youth. <u>His favorite hobby</u> was
   1   2   3

<u>collecting stamps</u>. I suspect <u>that now he may be tired of his youthful pastime</u>.
    4   5

His biggest collection in the old days, <u>stamps with pictures of African flora and fauna</u>,
                                         6

is now collecting <u>dust</u> in our attic. After <u>having it appraised by a stamp expert</u>, he says
            7   8

he is planning <u>to sell it</u>. I wonder <u>how much it's worth</u>.
         9   10

	Form	Function
1.	_____	_____
2.	_____	_____
3.	_____	_____
4.	_____	_____
5.	_____	_____
6.	_____	_____
7.	_____	_____
8.	_____	_____
9.	_____	_____
10.	_____	_____

Test Exercise 7.8

Identifying Form and Function

Directions: This exercise is similar to the previous one except that it is not confined only to nominals; it includes modifiers that you are familiar with. Identify each of the underlined elements according to both its form and its function. *Form* refers to word categories (noun, verb, preposition, etc.), names of phrases (prepositional phrase, noun phrase, gerund phrase, etc.), and clauses. *Function* refers to the specific role the word or word group plays in the sentence: subject, direct object, modifier of *run*, etc. Again, you'll find it helpful to picture the sentence on a diagram to figure out the function of the underlined item. [Answers are not given.]

Examples:	*Form*	*Function*
I think <u>that studying history is fascinating</u>.	nominal clause	dir obj
I think that <u>studying history</u> is fascinating.	gerund phrase	subject

1. My little brother enjoys <u>playing computer games</u>. _____ _____

2. Winning <u>computer</u> games gives him great satisfaction. _____ _____

3. Winning computer games gives <u>him</u> great satisfaction. _____ _____

4. <u>What he does with his time</u> is his own business. _____ _____

5. <u>What</u> he does with his time is his own business. _____ _____

6. <u>To get into a good law school</u> is not easy. _____ _____

7. Maria is planning <u>to go to law school in the fall</u>. _____ _____

8. Maria is planning to go to law school <u>in the fall</u>.

   _____ _____

9. I think that being <u>a lawyer</u> would be exciting.

   _____ _____

10. The elections <u>on our campus</u> rarely bring out many voters.

    _____ _____

11. The elections on our campus rarely bring out <u>many voters</u>.

    _____ _____

12. Many students <u>obviously</u> consider the student elections unimportant.

    _____ _____

13. Many students obviously consider <u>the student elections</u> unimportant.

    _____ _____

14. They do think <u>national elections are important</u>.

    _____ _____

15. They do think national elections are <u>important</u>.

    _____ _____

16. <u>Our friend from Tampa</u> spent last winter with us in Idaho.

    _____ _____

17. He often wondered <u>if winter would ever end</u>.

    _____ _____

18. He did enjoy <u>learning to ski</u>.

    _____ _____

19. <u>Skiing</u> is a good reason for living in Idaho.

    _____ _____

20. Skiing is also a good reason for <u>visiting Idaho</u>.

    _____ _____

Chapter 8

Sentence Modifiers

As you learned in Chapter 8 of *Understanding English Grammar,* the term **sentence modifier** refers to any word or word group that modifies the sentence as a whole rather than a specific part of it. Many sentence modifiers are parenthetical. As **independent words and phrases,** they are nearly always set off by a comma when they appear at the opening or closing of the sentence and by two commas when they appear in the middle:

> <u>Luckily</u>, I got a refund.

> Rap music bores me, <u>to tell the truth</u>.

> Shawn, <u>on the other hand</u>, loves it.

These parenthetical comments affect the pace of the sentence by slowing the reader down, by interrupting the main idea, or by shifting or focusing the reader's attention. The commas signal the reader that the word or phrase is an added comment, much like the nonrestrictive modifiers you saw in the discussion of adjectivals.

There are two other important classes of sentence modifiers. The **adverb clause** is connected to the main clause with a subordinating conjunction (such as *if, when, although, because*):

> <u>When I have time</u>, I will return your call.

The **absolute phrase**—a noun headword with a postnoun modifier, usually a participle—adds a detail about the sentence as a whole:

> <u>His voice trembling</u>, the valedictorian began his speech.

Exercise 8.1
Punctuating Sentence Modifiers

Directions: Add punctuation to the following sentences, if necessary.

1. The first act in my opinion was much too slow.

2. As the old saying goes you can lead a horse to water but you can't make him drink.

3. The storm unfortunately did a great deal of damage.

4. Luckily the power was out for only a short time.

5. Speaking of the storm did you notice all the trash cans overturned on the sidewalk this morning?

6. Another storm is on the way according to the latest weather report.

7. During our summer vacation I saw parts of the country I had never seen before.

8. Eastern Montana much to my surprise turns out to be absolutely flat.

9. For some reason I expected to see rolling hills there.

10. Western Montana on the other hand is filled with the spectacular scenery of the Rocky Mountains.

11. Glacier National Park for example is absolutely beautiful.

12. Seeing glaciers in the summertime was especially disconcerting.

Exercise 8.2

Using Subordinate Clauses

Directions: Turn the following complete sentences into subordinate clauses by (1) adding a subordinator in the opening position and (2) adding the resulting subordinate clause to another sentence as a modifier. You will have to supply the main clause. For a list of subordinating conjunctions, see page 75.

Example:

The party ended at midnight.

Because the party ended at midnight, we got home earlier than we had expected.

or

If the party ended at midnight, why didn't you get home before 3:00 a.m.?

1. Maxie slept until noon.

   _____

   _____

2. My books for this semester cost nearly a hundred dollars.

   _____

   _____

3. There was an explosion in the building across the street.

   _____

   _____

4. The Merced River flooded Yosemite National Park.

   _____

   _____

5. Drug use among professional athletes has been in the news again.

   _____

   _____

6. The new laws about food labeling should help people reduce their intake of saturated fats.

   _____

   _____

7. Several consumer groups are demanding ingredient labeling for alcoholic beverages.

   _____

   _____

8. The state of Nevada gets most of its revenue from the gambling industry.

   _____

   _____

9. The number of family farms in the United States continues to shrink with each passing year.

   _____

   _____

10. Fran can't decide whether to buy a pickup or a van.

    _____

    _____

ELLIPTICAL CLAUSES

An **elliptical clause** is a clause from which a word or words have been omitted, often the subject and part of the verb:

> While [he was] attending a play at Ford's Theater, President Lincoln was shot by John Wilkes Booth.

An elliptical clause will "dangle" when the omitted subject is different from the subject of the main clause:

> *Dangling:* When beginning a job search, the school's placement office can provide valuable advice.

To eliminate the problem of dangling, you can revise the main clause to make its subject match the implied subject of the elliptical clause:

> When beginning a job search, a student can get valuable advice from the university placement office.

Another solution to the problem is to write out the clause completely:

> When a student is beginning a job search, the university placement office can provide valuable advice.

Other problems with elliptical clauses are discussed in Chapter 8 of *Understanding English Grammar.*

Exercise 8.3
Recognizing and Revising Elliptical Clauses

Directions: Underline the elliptical clauses; then rewrite the sentences to eliminate their problems.

Example:

> <u>When studying for a test</u>, the first step is to psych out the teacher.
>
> When you are studying for a test, the first step is to psych out the teacher.

1. Before painting a car, the area should be free of dust.

   _____

   _____

2. I have discovered that many students don't study as hard as me.

   _____

   _____

3. Although hoping for good weather, the picnic tomorrow may, in fact, be rained out.

   _____

   _____

4. There was nothing of real value in all the trunks and boxes, when cleaning out the attic.

   _____

   _____

5. When doing an assignment at the last minute, your work will probably not be first-rate.

   _____

   _____

6. The price of gas in New Jersey is always cheaper than Pennsylvania.

   _____

   _____

7. While living in the Midwest, my Texas accent drew a lot of comments.

   _____

   _____

8. My sister's horse is older than her.

   _____

   _____

9. When delivering pizza to our apartment, it always arrives cold.

   _____

   _____

10. There was nothing to do while waiting for the rain to stop.

   _____

   _____

Exercise 8.4
Adding Absolute Phrases

Directions: Add an absolute phrase as a modifier to each sentence. Remember that an absolute phrase is a noun phrase in form—a noun headword with a postnoun modifier. The absolute will either focus on a detail of the whole or explain a cause or condition. It can either open or close the sentence.

Example:

The winning candidate moved to the center of the stage.

The winning candidate moved to the center of the stage, her hands clasped

triumphantly above her head.

1. The speaker droned on interminably.

   _____

   _____

2. Pat tried hard not to think about the needle in the nurse's hand.

   _____

   _____

3. The bear cubs rolled around in their cage.

   _____

   _____

4. The monkeys performed like trapeze artists for the children.

   _____

   _____

5. The desert looked beautiful in the moonlight.

_____

_____

6. The dessert looked sinfully delicious.

_____

_____

7. The losing candidate stood at the microphone to read a statement to the roomful of unhappy campaign workers.

_____

_____

8. Snoopy lounged on the roof of his doghouse.

_____

_____

9. The rain beat against the windshield.

_____

_____

10. The committee members began to argue among themselves.

_____

_____

Test Exercise 8.5

Form and Function

Directions: On the lines following each sentence, identify the underlined items according to both form and function. Remember that *form* refers to word categories (noun, verb, preposition, expletive, etc.), names of phrases (prepositional phrase, noun phrase, gerund phrase, infinitive phrase, participial phrase, etc.), and clauses (nominal clause, adverbial clause, relative clause, subordinate clause). *Function* refers to the specific role the word or word group plays in the sentence: subject, direct object, appositive, modifier of *play*, sentence modifier, etc. [Answers are not given.]

	Form	Function
1. <u>Clearly</u>, the wrong player was called for the foul.	_____	_____
2. I am positive, <u>Sir</u>, that you have made a mistake.	_____	_____
3. The fans considered that call <u>a real blunder</u>.	_____	_____
4. The fans hoped <u>that the referee would change his mind</u>.	_____	_____
5. <u>Getting a referee to admit a mistake</u> is impossible.	_____	_____
6. Getting a referee to admit a mistake is <u>impossible</u>.	_____	_____
7. <u>Their voices shaking the rafters</u>, the fans made a real difference in that game.	_____	_____
8. <u>If we had won the game</u>, we might have won the league championship.	_____	_____

9. If we had won that game, we might   _____   _____
   have won the <u>league</u> championship

10. <u>In truth</u>, winning that game   _____   _____
    would have been a great morale booster.

11. <u>Feeling cheated by the officials</u>,   _____   _____
    both fans and team were unhappy.

12. We threw a party after the game   _____   _____
    <u>to forget our disappointment</u>.

Chapter 9

Coordination

In the preceding chapters we have looked at various ways of expanding sentences by adding modifiers to nouns, to verbs, and to the sentence itself. In this chapter we will look at another kind of sentence expansion: **coordination**. To coordinate words, phrases, and clauses, we use three kinds of connectors:

1. Coordinating conjunctions: *and, or, but, yet, for*

2. Correlative conjunctions: *both-and, either-or, neither-nor, not only-but also.*

3. Conjunctive adverbs: *however, therefore, moreover, nevertheless, so, yet,* etc.

Understanding the various kinds of conjunctions will help you use compound elements effectively.

Exercise 9.1

Adding Coordinate Elements

Directions: Revise each of the following sentences by turning the underlined item into a compound, using the coordinating or correlative conjunction shown in parentheses.

Example:

The students <u>studied</u> until 3:00 A.M. (and)

The students studied and partied until 3:00 a.m.

_____

1. The children played <u>on the porch</u> all afternoon. (and)

_____

_____

2. I will work on <u>my math assignment</u> tomorrow. (either-or)

_____

_____

3. Pam <u>changed the oil</u> before leaving for spring break. (and)

_____

_____

4. Our teacher looked <u>cheerful</u> in class this morning. (yet)

_____

_____

5. Our visitors this weekend were <u>unexpected</u>. (but)

_____

_____

6. I <u>can</u> go with you to the police station. (and)

_____

_____

7. John can speak <u>Spanish</u> like a native. (both-and)

_____

_____

8. Juan can speak <u>English</u> like a native. (not only-but also)

_____

_____

9. My roommates are <u>going to San Diego</u> for spring break. (either-or)

_____

_____

10. I've decided <u>that majoring in math was a mistake</u>. (and)

_____

_____

PARALLEL STRUCTURE

As you read in Chapter 9 of *Understanding English Grammar,* an important consideration for coordinate elements is that they be parallel. A sentence is parallel when all of the coordinate parts are of the same grammatical form. The conjunctions must join grammatical equivalents, such as pairs of noun phrases or verb phrases or adjectives:

Noun phrases:	The university plans to build <u>a new library</u> and <u>three residence halls</u>.
Verb phrases:	They will also <u>remodel the administration building</u> and <u>repair the tennis courts</u>.
Adverbs:	<u>Swiftly</u> yet <u>gracefully</u>, Michele skated across the ice.
Prepositional phrases:	The line stretches <u>down the hall</u> and <u>out the front door</u>.
Nominal clauses:	I don't care <u>who you are</u> or <u>what you want</u>.

If you followed the instructions in Exercise 9.1, your coordinate elements should have turned out to be parallel.

Unparallel parts occur most commonly with the **correlatives**, the two-part conjunctions like *either-or* and *neither-nor.*

*For Kim's birthday present, I'll <u>either</u> buy a CD <u>or</u> a video.

It's easy to see the problem: The word group following *either* is a verb phrase; the one following *or* is a noun phrase. It's easy to correct the problem too. Just shift one part of the correlative pair so that both introduce the same kind of phrase:

I'll buy <u>either</u> *a CD* <u>or</u> *a video.* [noun phrases]

I'll <u>either</u> *buy a CD* <u>or</u> *rent a video.* [verb phrases]

Exercise 9.2

Revising for Parallel Structure

Directions: Rewrite the following sentences, paying particular attention to the unparallel coordinate elements.

Example:

My uncle's doctor told him to quit smoking and that he should start to exercise regularly.

My uncle's doctor told him to quit smoking and to start exercising regularly.

1. I just know the party will either be a big success or a total failure.

   _____

   _____

   _____

2. Either we will buy a second car or two bicycles for school transportation.

   _____

   _____

   _____

3. We were surprised when our history professor canceled class unexpectedly and that she gave us an extra week to write our term papers.

   _____

   _____

   _____

4. I am sure that a daily workout in the gym and going on a strict diet will give me a new shape before bikini season.

_____

_____

_____

5. Both hearing the judge's tone of voice and the look on his face made me nervous.

_____

_____

_____

6. What you do with your money and the way you spend your time are of no concern to me.

_____

_____

_____

7. You can either leave the car in the driveway or it can go in the garage.

_____

_____

_____

8. I heard on the news that the police have not only arrested a suspect in the robbery but he has confessed.

_____

_____

_____

9. Progressive education aims to teach students to be open-minded, thinking with logic, know how to make wise choices, having self-discipline and self control.

_____

_____

_____

10. The final step involves making a ninety-degree kick turn and then start the pattern over from the beginning.

_____

_____

_____

Exercise 9.3

Using Conjunctive Adverbs

Directions: Combine each pair of sentences into a compound sentence, using a conjunctive adverb in the second clause. Use a semicolon to connect the two clauses. Remember that the conjunctive adverb is movable; it need not introduce the clause. Among the common conjunctive adverbs are *however, therefore, moreover, nevertheless, so, thus, likewise, furthermore, consequently, yet,* and *in fact.*

Example:

Tires are no longer manufactured in Akron, Ohio.
The city still calls itself "The rubber capital of the world."

Rewrite: Tires are no longer manufactured in Akron, Ohio; nevertheless,

the city still calls itself "The rubber capital of the world."

1. The manager disagreed with the umpire's call.

   The team finished the game under protest.

   _____

   _____

2. Several trucks loaded with supplies drove up to the factory gates.

   The drivers refused to go farther and cross the picket line.

   _____

   _____

3. The winter vegetable crops were devastated by the flooding of Arizona's Gila River.

   Prices of lettuce and broccoli went sky high.

   _____

   _____

4. The chairman of the Planning Commission refused to allow our citizens' committee to present our petition.

   He ordered us to leave the meeting.

   _____

   _____

5. I have seen every episode of *Frasier* at least six times.

   I still enjoy watching them.

   _____

   _____

6. The new television season has been a real disappointment.

   Some of the programs are downright embarrassing.

   _____

   _____

7. The school board recently announced a possible deficit.

   The board is planning to spend over eighty thousand dollars on computers.

   _____

   _____

8. The city has established several new homeless shelters this year.

   Hundreds of the homeless still sleep on the streets and in the parks.

   _____

   _____

PUNCTUATION OF COORDINATE ELEMENTS

One of the positive outcomes of understanding grammar—especially the grammar of coordination—is the understanding of punctuation that comes with it. As you learned in Chapter 9 of *Understanding English Grammar,* there is an important difference between the punctuation of a compound sentence and a compound element within the sentence. When *and* joins a compound within the sentence, we use no comma:

> The mayor claims that the streets are clean <u>and</u> that they are safe.

Between sentences, however, we do use a comma with *and* when we join complete sentences:

> She also claims that the crime rate is low, <u>and</u> the latest figures support her claim.

Another possibility for joining the compound sentence is the semicolon, which we frequently use when a conjunctive adverb joins the two sentences:

> Violent crimes have decreased by 15 percent; <u>however,</u> burglary and auto theft are still on the rise.

We should note two additional punctuation conventions regarding compounding within the sentence:

1. When *but* is the conjunction, a comma is often called for to denote the contrast, or disjunction:

   The police have cracked down on crimes against people, <u>but</u> not on crimes against property.

2. In a series of three or more items, commas are called for between the parts:

   Crimes against people include murder, rape, robbery, <u>and</u> aggravated assault.

(Some writers regularly omit that last comma, the one before the *and* in a series.)

Exercise 9.4
Punctuating Coordinate Structures

Directions: Add punctuation to the following sentences—if they need it.

1. I took piano lessons for several years as a child but I never did like to practice.

2. When I started college I surprised both my mother and my former piano teacher by signing up for lessons and now I practice every spare minute I can find.

3. My hands are small however I have exercised my fingers and now have managed to stretch an octave.

4. My fingers are terribly uncoordinated but every week the exercises and scales get easier to play.

5. I was really embarrassed the first few times I practiced on the old upright in our dorm lounge but now I don't mind the weird looks I get from people.

6. Some of my friends even hum along or tap their feet to help me keep time.

7. I have met three residents on my floor who are really good pianists they've been very helpful to me when I've asked them for advice.

8. When I'm in my room studying I often play my collection of Glenn Gould records for inspiration.

9. I'm so glad that Bach and Haydn and Schumann composed music simple enough for beginners.

10. I'm looking forward to seeing the look on my mother's face when I go home at the end of the term and play some of my lessons from *The Little Bach Book* she will be amazed.

Chapter 10

Words and Word Classes

In the three chapters of Part IV in *Understanding English Grammar,* you took a close look at how words are formed and classified. You learned about morphemes, form-class words, structure-class words, and pronouns. The exercises in this chapter will give you further practice in understanding the grammar of words.

INFLECTION AND DERIVATION

As you learned in Chapters 9 and 10 of *Understanding English Grammar,* words are made up of **bases** and **affixes**. The base gives a word its primary meaning. An affix attached at the beginning is a **prefix**; one attached to the end is a **suffix. Inflectional** suffixes express some kind of grammatical information—like plural or past tense—but do not change the basic category of a word. English has only eight inflectional suffixes. They help us to identify the category of a word. We know *talked* is a verb, for example, because it has the suffix *-ed,* an ending that gets attached only to verbs.

  Derivational affixes, on the other hand, usually change the class of a word. For example, *educate* is a verb, but the addition of *-ion* turns it into a noun—*education.* All prefixes are derivational, and any suffix that's not inflectional will be derivational. English has numerous derivational affixes. We can sometimes identify a word because it ends in a particular derivational suffix. For example, words ending in *-ion* and *-ment* (*instruction, accomplishment,* etc.) are nouns; words ending in *-able* or *-ible* (*lovable, flexible,* etc.) are adjectives.

  The first six exercises in this chapter will give you practice in using inflectional and derivational affixes to analyze and classify words.

Exercise 10.1.
Derivational Suffixes

Directions: The words in the second column have been formed by adding a derivational suffix to those in the first column. Identify the class of the words in both columns: noun, verb, adjective, or adverb. Some words may belong to more than one class.

1. desire   desirable
2. false   falsify
3. day   daily
4. mouth   mouthful
5. ideal   idealize
6. ripe   ripen
7. real   realism
8. accept   acceptance
9. gloom   gloomy
10. race   racer
11. press   pressure
12. deep   depth
13. wind   windy
14. edit   edition
15. friendly   friendliness

Exercise 10.2

Using Bases and Affixes

Directions: Each of the following groups contains a base and some affixes, both derivational and inflectional. Make a word out of each group. Name the class of the word you have made.

Example:

-s, -ment, place, re-   replacements—noun

1. -less, care, -ly-   _____

2. -ed, light, -en   _____

3. -ize, -s, atom, -er   _____

4. -ing, -ate, termin   _____

5. -y, -er, grease   _____

6. re-, -en, sharp   _____

7. -dom, -ster, gang   _____

8. -s, -ist, organ   _____

9. -ate, -ive, act, de-, -s   _____

10. -ist, -ly, real, -ical   _____

11. -ly, -ion, -ate, affect   _____

12. province, -s, -ism,-ial   _____

13. be-, -s, little   _____

14. dis-, -ity, able, -es   _____

15. -ion, im-, -able, press   _____

HOMONYMS

Homonyms are words that have the same sound and the same spelling but have different meanings: *saw* (the tool) and *saw* (the past-tense verb). This same concept applies to morphemes—to parts of words that sound the same but have different meanings. The purpose of this exercise is to help you distinguish between suffixes that look and sound alike.

Exercise 10.3
Homonymic Suffixes

A. *Directions:* The suffix *-ly* is added to many adjectives to form adverbs of manner, as in *silent, silently; formal, formally; careful, carefully.* But this adverbial suffix has a homonym: the *-ly* that's added to some nouns to make them adjectives—*love, lovely; scholar, scholarly; man, manly; month, monthly.* This adjectival *-ly* is also used with some adjectives to derive a variation of the adjective with a different meaning: *sick, sickly.* Identify the following words as adverb or adjective; some may be both. Use each in a sentence to illustrate your classification.

Example:

softly (adverb)   The music played softly in the background. _____

1. falsely (_____)   _____

2. weekly (_____)   _____

3. cowardly (_____)   _____

4. deadly (_____)   _____

5. heavenly (_____)   _____

B. *Directions:* The *-er* suffix can be inflectional or derivational. As an inflectional suffix, we add it to adjectives to make the comparative form: *bold, bolder; happy, happier; cool, cooler.* As a derivational suffix, we add it to verbs to form nouns: *sing, singer; ride, rider; preach, preacher.* Identify the following words as nouns or adjectives. Use each in a sentence to illustrate your classification.

Example:

louder (adjective)   The music was louder than we expected. _____

1. heavier (_____)   _____

2. fighter (_____)   _____

3. tougher (_____)   _____

4. thriller (_____)   _____

5. producer (_____)   _____

HETERONYMNS

English has pairs of words that are spelled the same but differ in sound and meaning; they are called **heteronyms**. For example, when the word *does* is used as the plural of the noun *doe* (a female deer), it's pronounced to rhyme with *froze*; but when it's used as the third-person singular of the present tense for the verb *do* (as in "He does not see us"), it rhymes with *was*. Similarly, *lead* is the name of a metal (rhyming with *bed*) and also the verb meaning "to guide" (rhyming with *feed*). The following exercise will give you practice in spotting and distinguishing between these tricky pairs of words.

Exercise 10.4

Identifying Heteronyms

Directions: Each of the following sentences contains a pair of heteronyms. Pick them out, identify their word class, and define them.

Example:

The bass player had a bass painted on his t-shirt.

bass (n.) = a musical instrument; bass (n.) = a fish

1. The nurse wound the bandage around the wound.

2. My Polish friend Sophia wears black nail polish.

3. The wind was so strong that we couldn't wind up the string on our kites.

4. They shed a tear when they saw the big tear in their new couch.

5. The dove dove into the underbrush when we came down the path.

6. We told the garbage collector that he could not refuse to collect our refuse.

Now see if you can write sentences to illustrate the difference between these pairs: *present* and *present; row* and *row; sow* and *sow; object* and *object; close* and *close.*

Exercise 10.5
Form Classes and Inflectional Endings

Directions: The following words belong to more than one form class. Write sentences that demonstrate two classes for each word. Underline the word and label its class.

Examples:

room

> There are three <u>rooms</u> in our apartment.
>   noun

> My cousin <u>rooms</u> with three upperclassmen this year.
>   verb

warm

> Our hands got too <u>warm</u> when we <u>warmed</u> them over the fire.
>   adj   verb

1. watch

2. cool

3. kiss

4. dim

5. pitch

6. kind

7. love

8. light

9. tip

10. fast

Exercise 10.6

Identifying Form-Class Words

Directions: On the lines at the left, identify each underlined word as noun, verb, adjective, or adverb. You may have to consider position, markers, and function, as well as form, to make your classifications.

_____ 1. Most of the <u>freshmen</u> are envious of Carol's

_____ <u>athletic</u> ability.

_____ 2. The agile halfback <u>skillfully</u> avoided

_____ the charging <u>tackler</u>.

_____ 3. We arrived <u>late</u> and almost

_____ <u>missed</u> the introduction of the speaker.

_____ 4. The boss's <u>retirement</u> is expected at

_____ some <u>later</u> date.

_____ 5. He built a <u>better</u> mousetrap, but no

_____ one <u>bought</u> it.

_____ 6. We decided to <u>wallpaper</u> the kitchen

_____ with shiny <u>wallpaper</u>.

_____ 7. The party <u>backed</u> the right candidate

_____ in the <u>spring</u> election.

_____ 8. In April we will <u>spring</u> forward

_____ one <u>hour</u> for daylight-saving time.

_____ 9. The <u>evidence</u> in this case is

_____ quite <u>clear</u>.

_____ 10. They announced a new <u>round</u> of panel discussions,

_____ which will <u>round</u> out the conference.

_____ 11. 'Twas brillig and the <u>slithy</u> toves

_____ Did <u>gyre</u> and gimble in the wabe:

_____ All mimsy were the <u>borogoves</u>,

_____ And the mome <u>raths</u> outgrabe.

STRUCTURE-CLASS WORDS

In the previous exercises in this chapter, you identified and analyzed the components of **form-class words**—the nouns, verbs, adjectives, and adverbs that provide the lexical content in a sentence. In the following exercise you will be identifying and using **structure-class words**. These are the words that build grammatical structure rather than convey meaning.

The structure classes include *determiners, auxiliaries, qualifiers, prepositions, conjunctions, interrogatives, expletives,* and *particles.* They are called "structure-class words" because they supply the supporting structure for the form-class words. Unlike the form classes, the structure classes are relatively small and rarely add new members; and, with the exception of auxiliary verbs, they do not change form.

Exercise 10.7

Identifying and Using Structure Classes

A. *Directions:* Label the class of each underlined word.

Example:

    Trading stocks <u>on</u> the Internet <u>can</u> be <u>a</u> <u>very</u> risky venture.
              prep   aux   det qual

1. Mr. Wilson <u>has</u> remained <u>rather</u> quiet about <u>his</u> final decision.

2. <u>The</u> jurors were sequestered <u>for</u> weeks, <u>but</u> they <u>were</u> allowed to return home <u>after</u> the trial ended.

3. The family looked <u>on</u> in amazement <u>as</u> Lucille <u>very</u> carefully sprinkled olives <u>and</u> bacon bits on top <u>of</u> her ice cream.

4. <u>My</u> research group had <u>been</u> gathering information <u>about</u> prehistoric tribes in France.

5. <u>There</u> were <u>several</u> old friends who turned <u>up</u> unexpectedly at <u>Pat's</u> party.

6. <u>What</u> kinds of apples are <u>readily</u> available at <u>this</u> time of year?

7. The story <u>is</u> told about Winston Churchill that on <u>one</u> occasion <u>when</u> he was corrected for ending a sentence <u>with</u> a preposition he responded with something like, "This is the sort of nonsense up with which I <u>shall</u> not put."

B. *Directions:* Locate all the structure words in the following sentences; underline and label them as you did in Part A. The number in parentheses at the end of the item tells you how many structure words are in that sentence.

1. A résumé is a balance sheet without any liabilities. (4) [Robert Half]

2. The devil often cites Scripture for his purpose. (3) [Shakespeare]

3. She wears morals as a loose garment. (3) [Langston Hughes]

4. Any mother could perform the job of several air traffic controllers with ease. (6) [Lisa Alther]

5. In France cooking is a serious art form and a national sport. (4) [Julia Child]

6. By a small sample, we may know the whole piece. (4) [Cervantes]

PRONOUNS

Pronouns oil the wheels of good prose, helping avoid unnecessary repetition and moving a passage along smoothly. It's the writer's responsibility to make sure that each pronoun refers clearly to its **antecedent** (the noun it stands for). A pronoun with more than one possible antecedent can be puzzling. Pronouns can also be confusing if they do not refer to specific antecedents.

Exercise 10.8
Using Clear Pronouns

A. *Directions:* Examine the pronoun reference problems in the following passages. Then rewrite each passage to eliminate the problem. There may be more than one way to revise each passage.

Example:

> Clyde dropped his bowling ball on the patio and cracked it in three places.
>
> What does *it* refer to? The bowling ball or the patio?
>
> *Rewrites:* Clyde cracked his bowling ball in three places when he dropped it on
>
> the patio.
>
> Clyde broke the patio in three places when he dropped his bowling ball on it.

1. The client sued her broker after she had invested unwisely.

    _____

    _____

2. The detective removed the bloodstained shawl from the body and then photographed it.

    _____

    _____

3. Seth prepared three new proposals. He then spent an hour discussing them with the client. This probably kept the company from losing the account.

_____

_____

4. The company prohibited smoking, which annoyed some employees.

_____

_____

5. Maxine told Amy she thought she needed a vacation.

_____

_____

6. If you use the wrong cable to connect the printer to the computer, you may damage it.

_____

_____

B. *Directions:* On separate paper rewrite the following paragraph to get rid of all vague and ambiguous pronoun references. You may need to add words, take some out, or rearrange a few.

Myrtle and Marie were just finishing their second cup of coffee at Sandy's Country Kitchen when they told them they would have to leave. They complained that this wasn't fair, which they ignored. This made them furious, so she asked to speak to the manager, which proved to be a mistake. She came at once and told them that this wasn't a lounge; the restaurant was closing because they needed to go home. They protested that this was going to ruin its reputation for friendliness because they intended to tell all their friends about it. She said they could print it in the paper for all she cared, and then she turned on her heel and left them flabbergasted. Having no other recourse, they paid the bill and stomped out, vowing never to do it again.

Test Exercise 10.9
Identifying Word Classes

Directions: Identify the class of every word in the following sentences. Place your labels below the words: noun (n), verb (vb), adjective (adj), adverb (adv), determiner (det), auxiliary (aux), qualifier (qual), preposition (prep), conjunction (conj), expletive (exp), particle (part), pronoun (pro). [Answers are not given.]

Example:

   A clean glove often hides a dirty hand. (English proverb)
  det adj   n   adv   vb det adj   n

1.   Money will buy a pretty dog, but it will not buy the wag of its tail. [Josh Billings]

2.   One arrow does not bring down two birds. [Turkish proverb]

3.   If love is the answer, could you rephrase the question? [Lily Tomlin]

4.   There are no atheists on turbulent airplanes. [Erica Jong]

5.   Do not needlessly endanger your lives until I give you the signal.

   [Dwight D. Eisenhower]

6.   A little sincerity is a dangerous thing, and a great deal of it is absolutely fatal.

   [Oscar Wilde]

7.   History teaches us that we have never learned anything from it.

   [Georg Wilhelm Hegel]

8. A lot of parents pack up their troubles and send them off to camp.
[Raymond Duncan]

9. Throw a lucky man into the sea, and he will emerge with a fish in his mouth.
[Arab proverb]

10. I have written some poetry that I myself don't understand. [Carl Sandburg]

11. She never lets ideas interrupt the easy flow of her conversation. [Jean Webster]

12. He is a fine friend; he stabs you in the front. [Leonard Louis Levinson]

13. General notions are generally wrong. [Lady Mary Wortley Montagu]

14. The only difference between a rut and a grave is their dimensions.
[Ellen Glasgow]

15. When the insects take over the world, we hope they will remember our picnics
with gratitude. [Anonymous]

Chapter 11

Purposeful Punctuation

Chapter 15 of *Understanding English Grammar* summarizes the rules for using punctuation to mark boundaries, signal levels of importance, make connections, and add emphasis.

To make connections:

- Put a comma between independent clauses joined by a coordinating conjunction, but use a semicolon if the clauses already contain commas.
- Put a semicolon between independent clauses not joined by a coordinating conjunction.
- Put a semicolon between independent clauses when the second clause is introduced by a conjunctive adverb or adverb phrase.
- Put a colon between independent clauses if the second clause explains or amplifies the first one.

To signal levels of importance:

- Set off nonessential modifiers with commas.
- Set off interrupters with commas: transitional phrases, parenthetical comments, and nouns of direct address.
- Put a comma after introductory elements: prepositional phrases, one-word sentence modifiers, adverbial clauses and verb phrases, absolute phrases, and participial phrases.

To mark boundaries:

- Use commas to separate items in a series; use a semicolon if any of the items contain commas.
- Use a comma to separate coordinate modifiers of the same noun.
- Use a hyphen to join the elements of compound modifiers.

To add emphasis:

- Use a colon to introduce a list of appositives.
- Use dashes to highlight appositives, modifiers, and parts of compounds.
- Use parentheses to downplay explanatory or amplifying material.

The following exercises will give you practice in using punctuation for these purposes.

Exercise 11.1

Making Boundaries

Directions: The punctuation marks and capital letters have been removed from the following paragraph. Rewrite the passage to make it readable again by adding punctuation marks and capital letters. Do not add any words. The original version consisted of six independent clauses, marked by four capitals, four periods, two semicolons, five commas, one colon, one dash, and one hyphen.

punctuation one is taught has a point to keep up law and order punctuation marks are the road signs placed along the highway of our communication to control speeds provide directions and prevent head on collisions a period has the unblinking finality of a red light the comma is a flashing yellow light that asks us to slow down and the semicolon is a stop sign that tells us to ease gradually to a halt before gradually starting up again by establishing the relations between words punctuation establishes the relations between people using words

Pico Iyer, "In Praise of the Humble Comma"

Exercise 11.2
Signaling Levels of Importance and Adding Emphasis

A. *Directions:* Punctuate the following paragraph to make it readable and rhetorically effective. The original version included three commas and three dashes.

Most of the suspects were members of the Granger High School football team who had police said since June held up twenty-two fast-food restaurants and small retail stores. They were brazen police said they didn't even bother with masks. They were bold one or more allegedly carried a pistol to each crime. And they were braggarts as the robbery spree continued the boys apparently told their friends.

—Mark Miller, *Newsweek*

B. *Directions:* Add commas, semicolons, colons, and dashes to the following sentences.

1. Wealthy people in seventeenth-century Europe enchanted with tulips from the Middle East paid vast sums of money for one bulb in many cases the cost exceeded thousands of dollars.

2. Widely available at modest prices today tulips are still closely associated with the Netherlands the tulip however is not a native Dutch flower.

3. Like many other products in western Europe such as the potato and tobacco tulips came to Holland from another part of the world.

4. Most of the tulips probably originated in areas around the Black Sea in the Crimea and in the steppes to the north of the Caucasus.

5. A key figure in the history of European tulip interest is Carolus Clusius a botanist who had first achieved recognition for his work with medicinal herbs.

6. At Leiden's innovative hortus botanicus or botanical garden Clusius cultivated the bulbs and seeds of tulips thus introducing the flower to Holland.

7. The breeding of tulips with new color combinations had two important effects on the European primarily Dutch tulip market the new varieties such as the Semper Augustus which was white with red flames became exorbitantly priced and only the wealthiest aristocrats and merchants could afford them.

8. By the early 1630s however flower growers had begun to raise vast crops of simply colored tulips.

9. With more varieties and a greater price range tulips became one of the few luxury goods that could be purchased by members of all classes.

10. When the craze known as "tulip mania" reached its pinnacle in 1636-37 the practice of tulip speculation only relevant to prized varieties of the flower emerged.

11. Because growers could not sell tulips until they were ready merchants began issuing promissoory notes guaranteeing the future delivery of the bulb.

12. The key was to be able to resell the note before the tulip could be delivered the unlucky gambler was the person who could no longer resell the note because he now owned the actual tulip.

13. Today there are three popular varieties of tulips the Darwin which can be as large as a tennis ball and grows sixteen inches high the lily-flowered which has pointed petals and also grows tall and the parrot whose petals resemble feathers and which grows about seven inches high.

14. Cutting some varieties of tulips for display in a vase can be risky the cut flowers require a lot of water and if the supply is not replenished often the flowers quickly droop.

Answers to the Exercises

Answers to all exercise items are given for Chapter 1; for other chapters, answers are provided for odd-numbered items.

Exercise 1.1

1. Ring the bells loudly.

2. I gave my sister a book.

3. That Mary should stop smoking is clear.

4. Six tigers ran out of the jungle.

5. The ship sails today.
   Or: Ship the sails today.

6. My old green car runs well for its age.
   Or: For its age my old green car runs well.

7. She owns many beautiful antique birdcages.

Exercise 1.2

1. *descriptive:* describes the word order of NPs

2. *prescriptive:* gives advice about style

3. *descriptive:* describes the form of questions

4. *prescriptive:* warns against overuse of *be*

5. *prescriptive:* gives permission to use an informal expression

6. *descriptive:* describes the form of commands

7. *descriptive:* describes a structural feature of adverbs

8. *prescriptive:* warns against overusing the passive

9. *descriptive:* describes the form of past-tense verbs

10. *prescriptive:* gives advice about word choice

Exercise 1.3

1. I knew you weren't from New Jersey.

2. Eddie and he drove home very slowly.

3. We didn't do anything but listen to records.

4. We thought you had drunk all the ginger ale.

5. The children wanted to play by themselves.

6. She doesn't take it seriously because she doesn't believe in ghosts.

7. When they were in the planning stages, they underestimated the costs big-time. Or: They greatly underestimated the costs.

8. I can hardly believe what you said to the coach.

9. Sam and I won't be going to the game.

10. The boss asked Derek if he had done his cleanup.

Exercise 1.4

1. You are a cobbler, aren't you?

2. Why do you rejoice? What conquests does he bring home?

3. Do I dwell [or live] only in the suburbs of your good pleasure?

4. O mighty Caesar, do you lie so low?

5. This was the unkindest [or least kind] cut of all.

6. Do not think, you noble Roman, / That Brutus will ever go bound to Rome.

Exercise 1.5

1. *To sail* originally referred to use of the wind; now it's used for any ship regardless of the means of propulsion.

2. *To drive* originally meant "to push" or "to force"; now it can be applied to self-propelled vehicles (in the sense of guide or steer).

3. *Starve* once meant to die in any manner; now it means to die from lack of food.

4. *Meat* once referred to food in general (by contrast to drink); now it refers to the edible flesh of animals.

5. *Deer* used to mean any animal; it now refers to just one specific kind.

6. *Villain* once meant "farm laborer"; now it means "a wicked or evil person."

7. *Hussy* was once related to the word *housewife*; now it means "an immoral woman."

8. *Knave* once meant "male servant"; now it means "an unprincipled, crafty person."

9. *Lewd* used to mean "ignorant"; now it means "lustful" or "obscene."

10. *Knight* originally meant "a youth"; now it refers to a medieval soldier, the champion of a cause, or an honorary title.

Exercise 2.1

A1. *stays:* verb—present tense, -*s* form; other forms would be *stayed, staying*
    minutes: noun—plural -*s* ending; marked by determiner *thirty*

3. *icy:* adjective—derivational ending -*y*; comparative and superlative forms are *icier, iciest*
    supply: noun—marked by the determiner *an;* plural would be *supplies,* possessive would be *supply's.*
    huge: adjective—can be qualified (*very huge*); comparative and superlative forms would be *huger* and *hugest*

5. *mammals:* noun—plural -*s* ending; marked by determiner *these*
    often: adverb—no form clues, but means "how much" and can be moved in the sentence
    water: noun—marked by determiner *the:* plural would be *waters,* possessive would be *water's*

B1. The <u>young</u> <u>contestant</u> <u>seemed</u> very <u>nervous</u>.
           adj   N   V   adj

3. Some <u>raucous</u> <u>members</u> of the <u>audience</u> <u>laughed</u> too <u>loudly</u> at his <u>silly</u> <u>comments</u>.
          adj   N   N   vb   adv   adj   N

Exercise 2.2

1. (My) <u>relatives</u> have (many) odd <u>habits</u>.

3. (His) youngest <u>daughter</u> keeps (her) pet <u>ocelot</u> in (the) <u>kitchen</u>.

5. (Their) <u>father</u> bought (his) second <u>wife</u> (an) antique <u>cannon</u>.

7. (My) maternal <u>grandmother</u> dresses (her) three small <u>dogs</u> in sequined <u>sweaters</u>.

9. (Other) <u>people</u> sometimes have <u>trouble</u> with (these) weird <u>antics</u>.

Exercise 2.3

1. in our botany class [*adj*]; about her bird-watching project [*adj*]

3. of birds [*adj*]

5. On Tuesday mornings [*adv*]; from my study group [*adj*]; around the campus [*adj or adv*]

7. During the night [*adv*]; behind the garage [*adv*]

9. on television [*adj*]; with many viewers [*adv*]

Exercise 2.4

1. Rainfall | originates | in the ocean. (VI)
   | N | vb | prep phr |
   | subj | pred vb | adv |

3. The deepest part of the ocean | is | in the Marianas trench. (I)
   | NP | be | prep phr |
   | subj | pred vb | adv |

5. The water in the Dead Sea | is | extremely salty. (II)
   | NP | be | qualified adj |
   | subj | pred vb | subj comp |

7. Angel Falls in Venezuela | is | the world's highest waterfall. (III)
   | NP | be | NP |
   | subj | pred vb | subj comp |

9. Scientists | discover | many unusual creatures | in the ocean's depths. (VII)
   | N | vb | NP | prep phr |
   | subj | pred vb | dir obj | adv |

Diagrams:

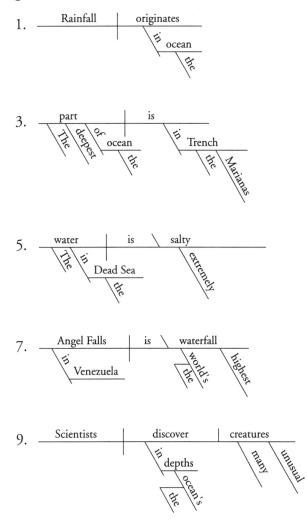

1. Rainfall | originates \ in ocean / the

3. part | is \ The deepest of ocean the in Trench the Marianas

5. water | is \ salty \ The in Dead Sea the extremely

7. Angel Falls | is \ waterfall in Venezuela world's the highest

9. Scientists | discover | creatures \ in depths ocean's the many unusual

Exercise 2.5

1. linking, pattern IV

3. linking, pattern IV

5. linking, pattern V

7. transitive, pattern VII

9. linking, pattern V

11. transitive, pattern VII

13. intransitive, pattern VI

15. intransitive, pattern VI

Exercise 2.6

Answers with diagrams:

1. In the first few decades of the twentieth century | Sears | sold | houses |
        prep phr   N   vb   N
          adv   subj   pred vb   dir obj

    through its catalogue. (VII)
        prep phr
         adv

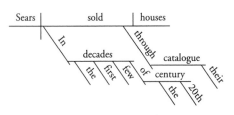

3. In 1992 | Sears | announced | the end of its catalogue sales. (VII)
   prep phr   N   vb   N
    adv   subj   pred vb   dir obj

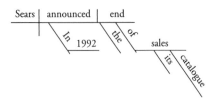

5. Apparently | our visitors from Reno | missed | their flight out of Chicago. (VII)
    adv   NP   vb   NP
                        subj   pred vb   dir obj

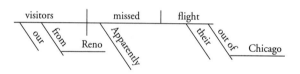

7. Adventure books | gave | me | endless hours of pleasure | during my childhood. (VIII)
        NP   vb   pro   NP   prep phr
        subj   pred vb   ind obj   dir obj   ADV

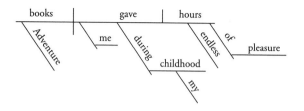

9. The service station attendant | simply | ignored | my pleas for help. (VII)
             NP   adv   vb   NP
             subj   pred vb   dir obj

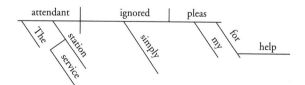

Exercise 2.7

1. The office | closes down | on the weekends. (VI)

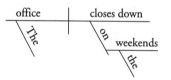

3. The wind | blew down | some trees. (VII)

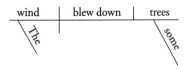

5. The bailiff | stood | by the door. (VI)

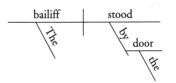

7. The defense | wrapped up | its case. (VII)

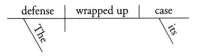

9. The judge | threw out | the verdict. (VII)

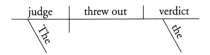

Exercise 3.1

1. was feeling: past + be + -ing + feel

3. may give: pres + may + give

5. have been working: pres + have + -en + be + -ing + work

7. had anticipated: past + have + -en + anticipate

9. can be: pres + can + be

Exercise 3.2

1. are studying

3. were being

5. have been helping

7. were working

9. could have been making

Exercise 3.3

1. pres + have + -en + repair [My car has been repaired by the mechanic.]

3. past + shall + give [The mechanic should probably be given a tip.]

5. pres + be + -ing + interview [All of the candidates are being interviewed by CBS tonight.]
   [Note: You could also say "on CBS."]

7. pres + be + -ing + call [The president's economic plan is being called a failure.]

9. past + can + have + -en + give [We could have been given a choice of several different term projects.
   Or: A choice of several different term projects could have been given to us.]

Exercise 3.4

1. Sidney Rosenthal invented the indelible marker in 1952. (VII)

3. The company sells more than a half a billion markers each year. (VII)

5. According to the National Graffiti Information Network, vandals cause four billion dollars in damage to public property annually. (VII)

7. The city of Lawrence, Massachusetts, banned marker sales to minors in 1985. (VII)

9. Binney & Smith, Inc., is now manufacturing Magic Markers. (VII)

Exercise 3.5

1. [A]The yearly bonus is really appreciated by the employees in my department.

3. [P] The government awarded our company a big contract.

5. [P] The company has invested our pension funds very wisely.

7. [A] I am considered very lucky because of my good job.

9. [P] The CEO and the Vice President should take a similar cut in extra pay.

Exercise 4.1

Sentence patterns:

1. (VI); 3. (VII); 5. (III); 7. (VII-passive); 9. (VIII)

Diagrams:

1. you | have been hiding
     Where

3. committee | Has raised | money
   the — *for* party *enough* — *the*

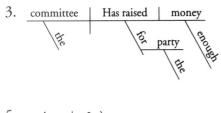

5. that | Is \ answer
   your *final*

7. assignment | should be done
   Which *first*

9. Prof. Watts | will give | essays
   When us *back* *our*

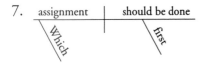

Exercise 4.2

Sentence patterns:

1. (VI); 3. (VII-passive); 5. (I); 7. (I); 9. (I)

Diagrams:

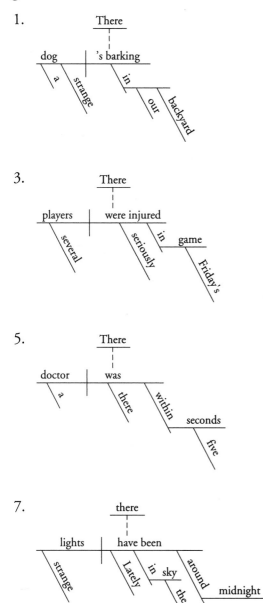

1.

Note: "in the sky" can also be interpreted as adjectival.

9.

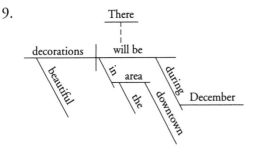

Exercise 4.3

1. It was negative political ads that turned off a great many voters in the last election.

3. It was in November 1992 that a fire in Windsor Castle caused over $100 million in damage.
   It was a fire in Windsor Castle that caused over $100 million in damage in November 1992.

5. It's in Branson, Missouri, that many country music stars have built their own theaters.

7. It was Ralph Nader's candidacy that changed the presidential election of 2000.
   It was the presidential election of 2000 that was changed by Ralph Nader's candidacy.

Exercise 4.4

These are some possibilities; you may think of others.

1. What caused the explosion was human error.

3. What bothers me about chemistry class is the poor condition of the lab equipment.

5. What you should ignore is his sarcasm.

7. What turns some people against politics is the enormous influence of lobbyists.

Exercise 5.1

1. In this part of the country, often, on summer evenings [*all modify* have]

3. How, happily, in winter, with so few hours of daylight [*all modify* do live]

5. According to recent estimates, during the past 300 years [*both modify* have become]

7. precariously, on the brink of extinction [*both modify* are teetering]

9. probably, not [*both modify* will make]

Exercise 5.2

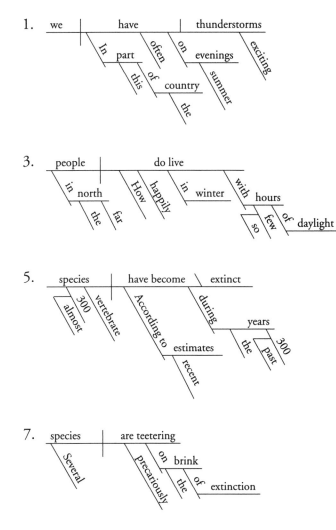

9.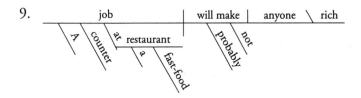

Exercise 5.3

1. At Mike's Halloween party [*prep ph*]; in the window [*prep ph*]; at midnight [*prep ph*]

3. to Florida [*prep ph*]; last year [*NP*]; when he retired [*clause*]

5. in this economy [*prep ph*]

7. To get to work on Monday [*inf ph*]; to work [*prep ph*]; on Monday [*prep ph*]

9. When you take the stairs [*clause*]; at every step [*prep ph*]

Diagrams:

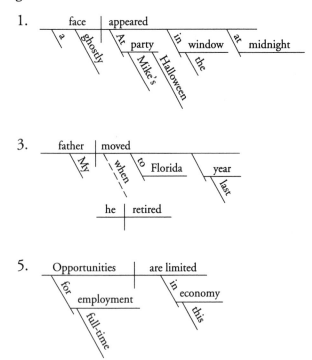

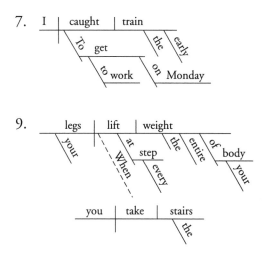

7. I | caught | train
   To get
   the early
   to work
   on Monday

9. legs | lift | weight
   your
   When
   at step
   the entire
   of body
   every
   your
   you | take | stairs
   the

Exercise 5.5

1. To keep the class happy [*inf*]

3. to graduate school [*prep—adv*]; to major in art history [*inf*]

5. To get detailed directions to Bryce Canyon [*inf*]; to Bryce Canyon [*prep—adj*]; to the Internet [*prep—adv*]

7. to the Constitution [*prep—adj*]; to a speedy and public trial [*prep—adj*]

9. To get on the waiting list for this class [*inf*]; to the academic vice-president [*prep—adv*]

Exercise 6.1

1. Several <u>students</u> in <u>my</u> math <u>class</u> have been absent since <u>the</u> midterm <u>exam</u>.
   indef   HW   poss   HW   art   HW
   pro   pro

3. In <u>my</u> <u>opinion</u>, <u>the professor's</u> strict attendance <u>policy</u> causes nervous <u>anxiety</u> in
   poss   HW   poss NP   HW   HW
   pro

   <u>many</u> <u>students</u>.
   indef   HW
   pro

5. <u>Many</u> <u>winners</u> of <u>this year's</u> Grammy <u>awards</u> are absolute <u>strangers</u> to me.
   indef   HW   poss NP   HW   HW
   pro

7. <u>My brother's</u> first (wife) now lives in (Denver).
    poss NP   HW   HW

9. <u>The</u> basketball (team) made <u>seven</u> three-point (shots) in <u>the</u> first (half) of <u>last night's</u> (game).
   art   HW   number   HW   art   HW   poss NP   HW

Exercise 6.2

1. across the hall [*adj*]; for everyone on our floor [*adv*]; on our floor [*adj*]

3. at the museum [*adv*]; for three hours [*adv*]; on Tuesday afternoon [*adv*]

5. of Vitamin A [*adj*]; in some people [*adv*]

7. on his porch [*adj*]; at a garage sale [*adv*]

9. For eight months [*adv*]; in the local school district [*adj*]; without a contract [*adv*]

Sentence patterns:

1. (VII); 3. (I); 5. (VII); 7. (VII); 9. (VI)

Diagrams:

1.
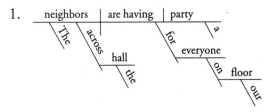

3.
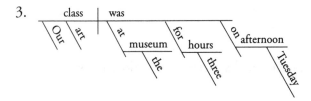

5.
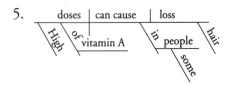

186

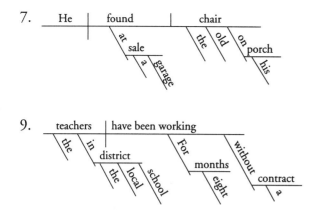

7.

9.

Exercise 6.3

1. Mitchell's novel, <u>which won the Pulitzer Prize in 1937,</u> sold over twenty million copies in thirty languages and forty countries.

3. The heroine of the story is Scarlett O'Hara, <u>who is a willful, defiant, manipulative Southern belle.</u>

5. After the death of her second husband, Scarlett finally marries Rhett Butler, <u>who is more than a match for her fiery nature.</u>

7. The movie <u>that was made from the novel</u> won ten Oscars and has become a classic.

9. Mitchell was born in Atlanta, <u>where she lived her entire life.</u>

Exercise 6.5

1. who is waving to us [*adj cl*]

3. who is a veteran of the Vietnam War [*adj cl*]; in Washington [*prep ph*]

5. in the Pacific Northwest [*prep ph*]; which always fluctuates with the economy [*adj cl*]; of the recession [*prep ph*]; that occurred in the late 1980s [*adj cl*]

7. who hates yard work [*adj cl*]; mowing the lawn [*part ph*]

9. where I was born [*adj cl*]

11. complaining loudest [*part ph*]; with the weakest credentials [*prep ph*]

Diagrams:

1.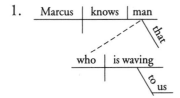

3.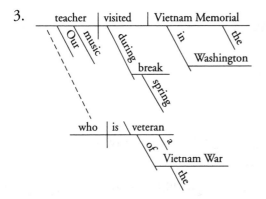

5.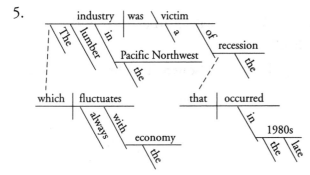

7.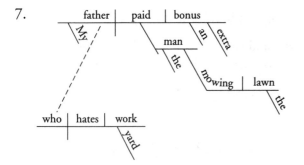

9.

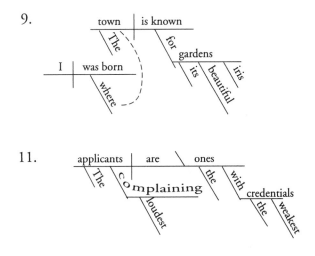

11.

Exercise 6.8

These are suggested revisions; you may come up with others.

1. Wearing her mother's wedding gown, Tanya walked down the aisle on her father's arm.

3. To understand the causes of arthritis and to find a cure for it, doctors are studying the disease extensively in medical laboratories throughout the country.

5. Rushing toward the railroad crossing, the train slowed down just in time to avoid a collision with the car stalled on the tracks.

7. Outdated and completely unworkable, the current Dormitory Visitation Policy is being revised by a joint committee of administrators, faculty, and student leaders.

9. Tracking further west than anticipated, Hurricane Ivan will reach the Florida coast by nine p.m., according to forecasters at the National Storm Center.

Exercise 6.9

Good rewrites may vary.

1. Everyday except Thursday, you are welcome to visit the cemetary where famous Russian artists and writers are buried.

3. The medical examiner determined the cause of death to be strangulation.

5. The Diamondbacks' starter was facing a batter who can knock over the fence any pitch he can reach.

7. Already legally blind, she was recently told by her doctors that her sight would soon be gone.

9. Jewel may be the first guitar-toting folksinger to take the stage in four-inch heels and a miniskirt.

Exercise 7.1

1. I have heard that the crew cut, the hallmark of the 1950s, is coming back in style.

3. The deepest part of the ocean, the Marianas Trench, is located in the Western Pacific near the island of Guam.

5. The paper nautilus octopus, a rare marine animal, lives in the coastal waters of Japan.

7. My sister's birthday, May 11, sometimes falls on Mother's Day.

9. During its annual migration, the golden plover, an amazing navigator, flies from the Arctic to Argentina.

Exercise 7.2, Step 1

1. winning the election in a landslide; to win the election in a landslide

3. losing her keys; to lose her keys

5. making too many mistakes on this biology homework; to make too many mistakes on this biology homework

7. giving the students an extra assignment; to give the students an extra assignment

Exercise 7.3

1. To keep the class happy [*adv inf*]

3. to graduate at the end of the summer [*nom inf*]

5. To get a good job with a decent salary [*adv inf*]; to have experience [*nom inf*]

7. to great lengths [*pp*]; to find that perfect job [*adv inf*]

9. to go to graduate school [*nom inf*]; to graduate school [*pp*]; to major in art history [*adv inf*]

Exercise 7.4

1. Where you spend your time [*subj*—VII]

3. that he's not very efficient [*subj comp*—II]

5. which movie we should rent [*dir obj*—VII]

7. Why you look so sad [*subj*—IV]

9. How I could have done so badly on the midterm [*subj*—VI]

Diagrams:

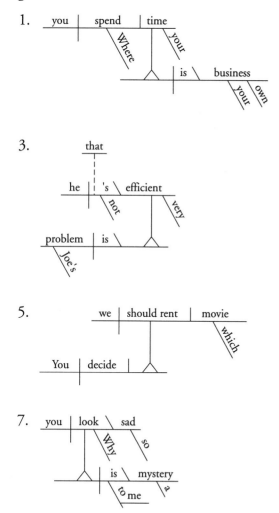

9.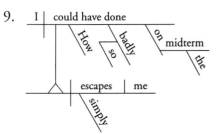

Exercise 7.5

1. before I heard the fire alarm [*adv—mod* smelled].

3. that people don't change [*nom—subj comp*]

5. that even if you win you're still a rat [*nom—subj comp*]; even if you win [*adv—mod* 're]

7. when you don't know where you are going [*adv-mod* will take]; where you are going [*nom-dir obj*]

9. who write clearly [*adj—mod* those]; who write obscurely [*adj—mod* those]

11. who like that sort of thing [*adj—mod* those]; they like [*adj—mod* thing]

Diagrams:

1.

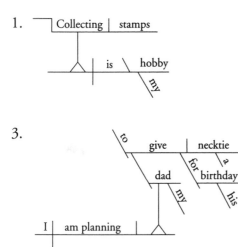

3.

5.

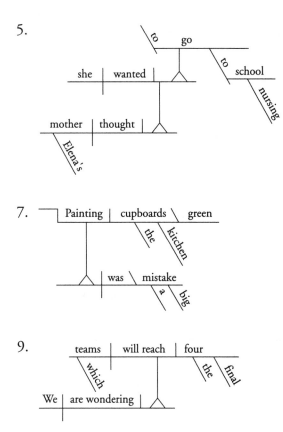

7.

9.

Exercise 7.7

1. NP, subject

3. NP, subject

5. nominal clause, direct object

7. N, direct object

9. infinitive phrase, direct object

Exercise 8.1

1. The first act, in my opinion, was much too slow.

3. The storm, unfortunately, did a great deal of damage.

5. Speaking of the storm, did you notice all the trash cans overturned on the sidewalk this morning?

7. During our summer vacation, I saw parts of the country I had never seen before.

9. For some reason, I expected to see rolling hills there.

11. Glacier National Park, for example, is absolutely beautiful.

Exercise 9.4

1. I took piano lessons for several years as a child, but I never did like to practice.

3. My hands are small; however, I have exercised my fingers and now have managed to stretch an octave.

5. I was really embarrassed the first few times I practiced on the old upright in our dorm lounge, but now I don't mind the weird looks I get from people.

7. I have met three residents on my floor who are really good pianists; they've been very helpful to me when I've asked them for advice.

9. I'm so glad that Bach and Haydn and Schumann composed music simple enough for beginners.

Exercise 10.1

1. desire—v[n]   desirable—adj

3. day—n   daily—adj [adv]

5. ideal—n [adj]   idealize—v

7. real—adj   realism—n

9. gloom—n   gloomy—adj

11. press—v [n]   pressure—n

13. wind—n [v]   windy—adj

15. friendly—adj   friendliness—n

Exercise 10.2

1. carelessly—adverb

3. atomizers—noun

5. greasier—adjective

7. gangsterdom—noun

9. deactivates—verb

11. affectionately—adverb

13. belittles—verb

15. impressionable—adjective

Exercise 10.3

The sentences are suggested examples.

A1. [adv]   Russ testified falsely.

  3. [adj]   It was a cowardly act.

  5. [adj]   Mona has a heavenly voice.

B1. [adj]   This coat looks heavier than it is.

  3. [adj]   This is a tougher test than the last one.

  5. [N]   Who is the producer of this film?

Exercise 10.4

1. wound (verb) = wrapped; wound (noun) = injury or cut

3. wind (noun) = air movement; wind (verb) = coil or roll up

5. dove (noun) = a bird; dove (verb) = past tense of "dive"

Exercise 10.5

1. noun, verb
3. noun, verb
5. noun, verb
7. noun, verb
9. noun, verb

Exercise 10.6

1. noun, adjective
3. adverb, verb
5. adjective, verb
7. verb, noun
9. noun, adjective
11. adjective, verb, noun, verb (or noun)

Exercise 10.7

A1. aux, qual, det
3. part, conj, qual, conj, prep
5. exp, det, part, det
7. aux, det, conj, prep, aux
B1. <u>A</u> (det), <u>a</u> (det), <u>without</u> (prep), <u>any</u> (det)
3. <u>her</u> (det), <u>as</u> (prep), <u>a</u> (det)
5. <u>In</u> (prep), <u>a</u> (det), <u>and</u> (conj), <u>a</u> (det)

Exercise 10.8A

Good answers may vary.

1. The client, who had invested unwisely, sued her broker.
   The client sued her broker, who had invested unwisely.

3. Giving the client more choices probably kept the company from losing the account.
   Taking the time to explain the proposals probably kept the company from losing the account.

5. Maxine told Amy, "I think I need a vacation."
   Maxine thought Amy needed a vacation and told her so. Or: Maxine told Amy, "I think you need a vacation."

Exercise 10.8B

Here is an acceptable rewrite, with the changes underlined. Your revisions may vary.

Myrtle and Marie were just finishing their second cup of coffee at the Kozy Kitchen, when <u>a waitress</u> told them they would have to leave. <u>The surprised customers</u> complained that <u>they were not being treated fairly</u>, but <u>the waitress</u> ignored them. This <u>failure to respond</u> made them furious, so <u>Myrtle</u> asked to speak to the manager, <u>a request that</u> proved to be a mistake. <u>The manager</u> came at once and told <u>the two women</u> that <u>they were not in a lounge</u>; the restaurant was closing because <u>the help</u> needed to go home. <u>Myrtle and Marie</u> protested that this <u>incident</u> was going to ruin <u>the restaurant's</u> reputation for friendliness because they intended to tell all their friends about <u>being ordered to leave so rudely</u>. <u>The manager</u> said <u>Myrtle and Marie</u> could print <u>their complaint</u> in the paper for all she cared, and then she turned on her heel and left them flabbergasted. Having no other recourse, <u>the irate customers</u> paid the bill and stomped out, vowing never to <u>eat at the Kozy Kitchen</u> again.

Exercise 11.1

Here is the way the original was punctuated:

Punctuation, one is taught, has a point: to keep up law and order. Punctuationi marks are the road signs placed along the highway of our communication—to control speeds, provide directions, and prevent head-on collisions. A period has the unblinking finality of a red light; the comma is a flashing yellow light that asks us to slow down; and the semicolon is a stop sign that tells us to ease gradually to a halt before gradually starting up again. By establishing the relations between words, punctuation establishes the relations between people using words.

Exercise 11.2

A. Here is the original version:

Most of the suspects were members of the Granger High School football team who had, police said, since June held up twenty-two fast-food restaurants and small retail stores. They were brazen—police said they didn't even bother with masks. They were bold—one or more allegedly carried a pistol to each crime. And they were braggarts—as the robbery spree continued, the boys apparently told their friends.

B.

1. Wealthy people in seventeenth-century Europe, enchanted with tulips from the Middle East, paid vast sums of money for one bulb; in many cases the cost exceeded thousands of dollars.

3. Like many other products in western Europe, such as the potato and tobacco, tulips came to Holland from another part of the world.

5. A key figure in the history of European tulip interest is Caroulus Clusius, a botanist who had first achieved recognition for his work with medicinal herbs.

7. The breeding of tulips with new color combinations had two important effects on the European "primarily Dutch" tulip market: The new varieties such as the Semper Augustus, which was white with red flames, became exorbitantly priced; and only the wealthiest aristocrats and merchants could afford them. [Some writers would not capitalize "the" after the colon.]

9. With more varieties and a greater price range, tulips became one of the few luxury goods that could be purchased by members of all classes.

11. Because growers could not sell the tulips until they were ready, merchants began issuing promissory notes guaranteeing the future delivery of the bulb.

13. Today there are three popular varieties of tulips: the Darwin, which can be as large as a tennis ball and grows sixteen inches high; the lily-flowered, which has pointed petals and also grows tall; and the parrot, whose petals resemble feathers and which grows about seven inches high.

NOTES

NOTES

NOTES

NOTES

NOTES

NOTES